Arts Institute at Bournemouth / Alberta C
rjah / Art Center College of ... li
logna / Boston University, School of Visual
Brigham Young Univer... Arts Academ
Art and Design ... rica, the Ber
ol of Logic and Ma... ellenbosch Unive
f Technology / Istanbul Bilgi University /
e / Massachusetts College of Art and Desi
e University / The University of the Arts /
r / Folkwang University Essen / Rhode Isla
the Art Institute of Chicago / Senac Unive
esign / School of Visual Arts, MFA / Swinb
yler School of Art / Royal College of Art /
tá Jorge Tadeo Lozano / Autonomous Me
oa / University of Technology / The Unive
Washington, School of Art / University of V
sity of the Applied Arts / Hongik Universit
hool of Visual Arts / Maryland Institute Co
ndon College of Communication / Univer
/ Alberta College of Art and Design / An
f Design / Berlin University of the Arts / A
School of Visual Arts / Suzhou Art and

DESIGN SCHOOL

BEVERLY MASSACHUSETTS

ROCKPORT PUBLISHERS

CONFIDENTIAL

Extraordinary Class Projects from
International Design Schools

* Steven Heller & Lita Talarico *

First published in the United States of America by
Rockport Publishers, a member of
Quayside Publishing Group
100 Cummings Center
Suite 406-L
Beverly, Massachusetts 01915-6101
Telephone: (978) 282-9590
Fax: (978) 283-2742
www.rockpub.com

Library of Congress Cataloging-in-Publication Data
Heller, Steven.
   Design school confidential : extraordinary class projects from international design schools/
   Steven Heller, Lita Talarico.
      p. cm.
   ISBN-13: 978-1-59253-548-4
   ISBN-10: 1-59253-548-8
1. Graphic arts—21st century. 2. Design–History—21st century. 3. Graphic arts—Study and teaching (Higher) 4. Design—Study and teaching (Higher) I. Talarico, Lita. II. Title. III. Title: Extraordinary class projects from international design schools.
NC1000.H44 2009
745.4071'1--dc22   2009014431
                                                                          CIP

ISBN-13: 978-1-59253-548-4
ISBN-10: 1-59253-548-8

10 9 8 7 6 5 4 3 2 1

Design: Landers Miller Design

Printed in China

acknowledg-
ments

THIS BOOK WOULD NOT BE POSSIBLE if not for our colleague Lara McCormick, whose organizational skills were put to the test. Thanks also to Hyun-Jung Hwang, Jia Chen, Lesley Weiner, and Zarina Lagman for their invaluable assistance.

Much gratitude goes to our tireless editor at Rockport, Emily Potts, the chief shepherd of this material, and to art director Regina Grenier.

A book is often as good as its design, and our designer Rick Landers, who produced a brilliant format, has been essential to the creative team. A big tip of the hat to Esther Ro-Scofield and Matthew Shapoff, at the School of Visual Arts, MFA Designer as Author program, for helping with our technical needs.

We appreciate the continued support of David Rhodes, President, and Anthony Rhodes, Vice President of the School of Visual Arts.

Thanks to all the teachers and students who contributed so generously to the development of this project. —SH + LT

→ contents:

Introduction

The Gold Standard

EXTRAORDINARY CLASS PROJECTS are worth their weight in gold (assuming one can actually weigh a class project). Those projects that, for years after they are done, students discuss and teachers imitate are essential to a successful design education. Truly challenging projects separate the wheat from the chaff, weak from strong, competent from genius. They can be both frightening and tantalizing—and are known to cause sleepless nights and stressful days. Projects are, of course, conceived in various ways to suit different needs: Some are offered just once, while others are assigned year after year until their educational usefulness comes to an end.

In the annals of design pedagogy, a few seminal projects stand out, usually associated with preeminent teachers. Some of the most well known are Edward Fella's found object collage project, Dan Friedman's weather report project, Emil Ruder's Basel typography exercise, Wolfgang Weingart's nonfunctional design elements project, and Stefan Sagmeister's "Touch Someone's Heart" project. Many of these "branded" projects evolved over time and belong to their creators much as their individual styles or manners are key to their design personas. Yet the most successful projects are not just ego trips for the teachers; they are intensive challenges that force students to go beyond perfunctory solutions to find a catharsis that offers greater

knowledge, understanding, and perhaps even wisdom. Occasionally, a unique class project can trigger a sea change in overall style or technique.

One such shift occurred with the "Vernacular Message Sequence," an annual project that Katherine McCoy assigned to Cranbrook Academy of Art graduate students from 1975 to 1995 when she was co-chairperson. The proposition was simple: It began with basic typographic grid exercises (highly rational and analytical, based on exercises by Emil Ruder and Dan Friedman) and progressed sequentially toward interpretive steps using imagery and vernacular elements. One of the most memorable solutions came in 1984 when Robert Nakata transformed the Heinz Ketchup label by reinterpreting and reconfiguring the common graphic elements that comprise the ubiquitous commercial label. Nakata retained the most identifiable characteristic—the keystone shape—but deconstructed the rest of the typography, resulting in an array of virtually abstract forms. In reconceiving something so familiar, the students learned what was essential to the identity of the design, what could not be tampered with lest it be forever altered, and what was expendable. It was also a lesson in how mutable even the most well-known designs can be and still retain some shred of identity. But, more significant, in do-

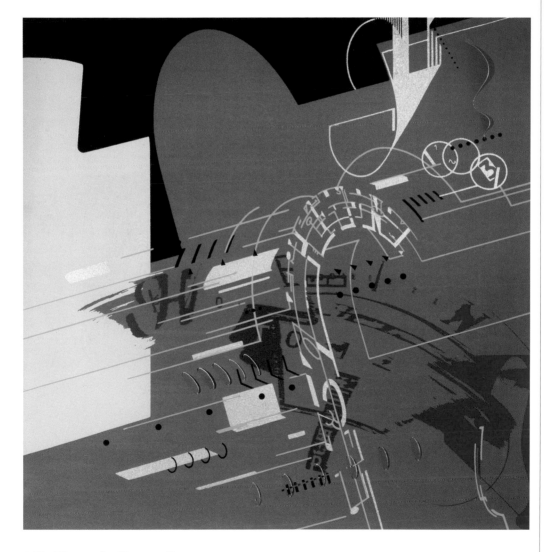

↑ The Vernacular Message Sequence

Heinz Ketchup logo by Robert Nakata based on exercises by Emil Ruder and Dan Friedman

ing this class project, Nakata inadvertently produced an icon of the new wave or postmodern design era that has been reproduced in various design history books as exemplary of that period, "Nakata's project definitely broke more new ground than most," recalls McCoy, who continued to assign the project sequence for another decade.

McCoy found that this project was the perfect opportunity for student participation because each year they introduced new demands on it: "The really big standout sequence in those last years at Cranbrook was by Andrew Blauvelt for his Tide detergent package. Andrew pointed out that the sequence was ending in expressive abstraction. He wanted to add imagery's symbolic content and narrative. I found this was a great perception, and so we included some steps that added imagery in the place of the abstract forms to build a story. Andrew did it the best. His perception prompted me to develop an additional section to the project sequence that focused on narrative, and it became much more meaningful with that addition. The moral to this story—it's important to listen to great students, respond to their ideas, and build on them. In the end, the teacher always learns the most." A well-conceived project is packed with opportunities for growth on both sides of the bifurcated brain.

While testing the mettle of the student, the best briefs lay the foundation for solid professional behavior. Even the most eclectic ones should impart lessons that can be used in future practice. Therefore, a project should not be seen as an end in itself, but as a steppingstone leading to a larger experiential goal. In the long and short run, it is not enough to solve the problem simply to receive a passing grade. The outcome of a project has more value; communally speaking, it enables everyone in a class to learn from the successes *and* the failures. School projects are integral to the growth process. So understanding how and why design schools and programs, both undergraduate and graduate, develop their projects is critical.

Design School Confidential surveys over fifty astute and eclectic projects emanating from as many international schools. While the customs and languages of these schools vary, the design languages and often the educational goals are extremely similar. Different countries may have their own cultural or commercial reasons for how graphic design is used, but the fundamentals are the same the world over. However distinctive the project, it has the potential to bridge cultural differences.

The projects in this book were selected carefully to fulfill this mission; yet had more projects been sampled, the majority would

↑ **The Vernacular Message Sequence**
Tide detergent package by Andrew Blauvelt

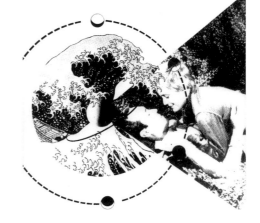

likely be fairly similar. The primary mission of every design degree program is to teach design literacy. So class projects are usually intended to exercise typographic or conceptual muscles, and these do not diverge too widely from a particular standard approach. No matter where in the world a school is located, most type classes teach the same fundamental skills and knowledge—it would be foolish to do otherwise. Owing to the widespread dissemination of design trends and styles through trade journals and websites, the world is a smaller place when it comes to type and typography. At a certain point in every student's education, however, it is essential to break from conventional methodologies, if only to emphasize that for creativity to prosper, rules must be broken. Too much rule-bashing can, of course, be overkill; projects that at once teach effective techniques and encourage unconventional thinking are needed to instill in students the reality that graphic design is a balance between old and new, conservative and eccentric, safe and dangerous.

The class projects chosen in *Design School Confidential*, therefore, do not conform to one specific dominant style or method, but the majority do have one thing in common: social context. Many educators agree that teaching type and image without providing a real-world context is like driving a car on a long stretch of straight highway—it is safe and boring, and the driver learns very little. Conversely, a good class project is like dealing with all the hazards of the road in an automobile simulator—safe, but challenging—while a truly great class project is like navigating a really treacherous road in a real car without airbags. Although the student is protected to some extent by the walls of academe, when given a real-world project with variables, limitations, and consequences, the results are decidedly less rarified. Many of these projects were selected because the teachers removed the airbags, and the students showed courage and ingenuity.

The goal of this book is not merely to exhibit interesting work, although it is all indeed exemplary; surveying class projects from around the world reveals the common as well as the distinctive characteristics that will contribute to a greater understanding of design and how to educate its practitioners. But these lofty pursuits aside, just the sheer level of creativity by these students is pretty extraordinary. Doubtless all teachers look forward to the presentation of class projects because that's when the great ideas percolate—and when they learn which students are, in fact, worth their weight in gold. ■

Section 1

Anatomy of a Successful Project

The Teacher's Perspective

WHEN ASKED TO ASSESS THE GOALS and expectations of their respective class projects, a dozen design teachers all agreed (regardless of grade or experience level) on three desired outcomes. First, challenge the student: A project must offer sufficient variables and serendipity that students can test their skills and talents and, in the final analysis, surprise both their teacher and themselves. Second, inform the student: A project must also provide enough unanswered questions that students are learning something new by doing something new. Third, elevate the student: A project can propel students in two opposing directions—either through success or failure. While the former is obvious, the latter way might seem perplexing. Often, however, only through failure can a student get the best critique and truly absorb the right lessons. Although failure will not produce a great portfolio piece, it can have a longer-term influence. *Challenge, inform,* and *elevate* are the building blocks of a solid education, and to achieve this mix requires a selfless devotion on the part of the teacher and an intense willingness to learn

on the part of the student. A good, or great, class project can make the educative experience real.

Yet from a teacher's perspective, there is a further outcome: a uniquely absorbing project that is talked about and anticipated over time, becoming legendary among students and teachers alike, and a veritable signature for that teacher. Legendary class projects are perennial (they never seem to become dated) because the process and results are so enlightening. More than a few storied projects from some well-known design instructors have garnered such status. In the 1960s, for example, Milton Glaser and Henry Wolf had students in their School of Visual Arts publication class produce an entire magazine of their choosing, and while this may seem de rigueur today, then it was a novel approach to teaching publication design by making the students editors as well. The project fostered community while highlighting the strengths (and, of course, the weaknesses) of the participants.

A project of this kind becomes celebrated because, like any essential resource of knowledge or experience, it triggers expectations in the student and in the teacher. It is as though doing this one special assignment will alter the course of a student's career—for the better and forever. This should not suggest, however, that only legendary projects can achieve such a goal, for even the most routine assignments can indelibly affect a student's understanding or appreciation of design. And these projects, although not storied, are just as important.

All teachers assign focused projects that address key facets of their particular classes. Designing a book cover series makes sense for a typography class; designing music videos is appropriate for a motion design class, and so on. But increasingly, even introductory and intermediate design teachers are introducing less predictable, more customized projects to both challenge the student and prompt them to adapt to real-world problems.

What ultimately determines whether a project is highly effective is how it best shapes the collective design experience. Ideally, it should follow the equation: a. skill or talent + b. conceptual acuity = c. increased level of performance. A superb customized project does all of the above yet also enlightens. If well planned, a project will also encourage interaction and collaboration so that students learn not just from the demands of the project (or the dictates of the teacher), but from each other. A teacher must provide the parameters and then critique the result, yet working with one's peers to shape a unique conclusion is at least 50 percent of the problem solving.

A good class project is combustible, it is the fuel that powers the creative engine; or put less metaphorically, it is the beginning, not the end, of an experience. It must lead to other results beyond the scope of a particular class; it must lead to the next educative level. Of course, context is everything. Presumably, projects aimed at freshmen or sophomores will be more basic than those for juniors or seniors, while those for graduate students will be more complex and nuanced. This does not mean that a sophomore project needs to be more pedestrian than a senior one. The teacher's responsibility at every level is to engage the students with problems (and then add twists to those problems).

DESIGNING A GREAT CLASS PROJECT

ONE OF THE MOST DIFFICULT JOBS a teacher faces—in addition to imparting knowledge, which is no small feat—is to design an inspiring class project. Although anyone can devise a quiz on the spur of the moment, a well-considered project is akin to writing a scenario with a beginning, middle, and end. The teacher must anticipate the response while allowing license so that students can interpret or reinterpret the brief. The veteran teacher may have seen all the answers at one time or another, but if the project is nuanced enough, surprise is built into the end product.

So how is a project conceived? After discussing the process with various teachers, consensus emerges. The most important questions are How will the project encourage learning? and What lessons are essential to learn? If the class is about packaging, for instance, the project must allow the students to tap into the theoretical knowledge they have acquired over the course of a semester and transform that into practical action. Some packaging projects emphasize labeling while others focus on sustainable materials; some are concerned with new forms others are limited to existing ones. The intended outcome dictates the demands of the project.

Basic projects—including ones devoted to typographic fluency, image manipulation, or color theory—have fairly obvious rationales. But more venturesome projects that involve a number of variables—the kinds that students wonder why they must do—are less overt. Here, a few teachers from the School of Visual Arts in New York speak to how and why they designed their unique projects:

Allan Chochinov

The Pooper Scooper Project

MFA DESIGN, SCHOOL OF VISUAL ARTS, NEW YORK, NEW YORK, USA

Briefly describe your class project.
Designing a pooper scooper is a great project to assign as an icebreaker at the start of the semester. It's silly and irreverent, and appears to be easily solvable. Very quickly though, students discover that there's much more to the problem than they originally thought: Beyond the ergonomic and mechanical issues is a world of discovery around public health, community, compliance, personal hang-ups, convenience, and caregiving. It's a dumb little problem with huge possibilities.

What inspired this project?
Truth be told, I actually worked on a pooper scooper project early in my professional career. At the studio we decided that for the project to be deemed a success, we'd shoot for getting it into the MoMA store. Alas, it was no-go: They refused to have any pet products in the line in those days. (Now there are plenty.)

What do you hope to get from the students who do this project?
I've found a lot of design students to be function obsessed, seldom considering issues larger than the mechanics of an object itself. This project is a real Trojan horse; it challenges designers to solve a relatively unsolvable problem—it's very hard to beat a plastic bag—and very quickly moves them into strategy, systems thinking, ethnography, anthropology, and sustainability.

What are the surprises that emerge from the project?
I'd have to say that I am forever stunned at the solutions that come out of this problem. The diversity is amazing, and many of the solutions have become iconic for me in terms of design thinking and pedagogical payoff.

You've assigned the project for some time; how has it changed?
Well, I'm not sure the problem has changed, but I have changed. It's important never to pigeonhole a student's work, of course, even if it's something you've seen before. The project serves as a reminder to me to always honor their efforts and individual approach. The problem is always new to them.

Has it met your expectations?
My expectations are consistently surpassed by students, regardless of the assignment. That's one of the best things about teaching.

From left to right: pooper scooper process sketches; poop replicas; investigating the current scoop options on the market

James Victore

The Urban Studio

ADVERTISING AND DESIGN, SCHOOL OF VISUAL ARTS, NEW YORK, NEW YORK, USA

↑ Stencil

Student: Krzysztof Piatowski

↑ Yard Sale

Student: Victoria Abrami

Briefly describe your class project.

The class is billed as the Urban Studio. The mission is for students to do finished work, unbridled by commercial constraints, and get it out to a real audience in New York City. Initially, we devised the class as an outlet for students to get a taste of realizing their work in its fullest form—and wanting more. But it has actually turned into a class about bravery. We push the students into situations where graphic design alone won't serve them—they have to interact with the public, and it changes the intention into something much more than expected.

What inspired this project?

Frustration! I was frustrated with commercial venues, as well as with advising seniors on their portfolios.

What do you hope to get from the students who do this project?

I hope they will get further excited by graphic design.

What are the surprises that emerge from the project?

Since part of the class is out of the classroom, very unexpected things happen. The accidental collaborations with other students, cops, the homeless, and New Yorkers make great surprises. We recently had a student giving free hugs for twenty minutes; the response was real and human and great, as well as unexpected. Another student created a bubble blowing experience in Union Square that at one point involved maybe seventy to one hundred people.

You've assigned the project for some time; how has it changed?

I get better at it.

Has it met your expectations?

Maybe. My expectations are really high. Maybe I need to wait and see what kind of professionals these students become.

↑ Free Hugs

Student: Da Won Chung

Richard Poulin

Visual Storytelling and Narrative Form

ADVERTISING AND DESIGN, SCHOOL OF VISUAL ARTS, NEW YORK, NEW YORK, USA

Briefly describe your class project.
Two class projects are entitled "Visual Storytelling and Narrative Form." In these assignments, the student is given either a play (Tony Kushner's *Angels in America: Millennium Approaches*) or a poem (Maya Angelou's "On the Pulse of Morning") to read, analyze, and visually interpret with typography and photographic imagery. Both of these narratives, while extremely different in form, share the use of symbolism, metaphor, and rich, descriptive narrative elements.

Play: The students have to conceptualize photographic imagery that visually communicates their point of view and interpretation of the play's theme(s). They are limited to photographic imagery composed entirely with a camera. This limitation provides students with an opportunity to further develop their own discipline and language for conceptualizing imagery without their reliance on a computer or image manipulation software. Typography, color, composition, etc., are then developed as supporting, interpretive elements to their photographic imagery. The final elements are developed into a theatrical poster for a production of the play.

Poem: A similar conceptual approach, as outlined above, is taken with the poem's narrative; however, the student's final solution takes the form of a book. The student is required to develop a concept relying on both interpretive typography and photographic imagery that visually communicates their point of view in response to the poet's words, metaphors, symbols, and themes. Imagery in this design problem is based on the student's research of American photographers (e.g., Evans, Cunningham, Callahan, Goldin, Mapplethorpe, Siskind, Fink) and using selected photography as meaningful and effective visual elements to further clarify and strengthen their interpretation of the narrative.

↑ **Angels in America poster**
Designer: Joshua Carpenter

↑ **Angels in America poster**

Designer/Photographer: Andrew Schoonmaker

What inspired these projects?

In both situations (that is, when I first saw the play as well as read the poem), they immediately influenced the way in which I related to, and valued, the written word as a designer. Both narrative forms rely upon the reader's imagination. They allow the reader to arrive at a very personal point of view in response to the writer's words. I knew that at some point I would be using these narratives for class assignments, hoping my students would have a similar response and be inspired in a similar way.

What do you hope to get from the students who do this project?

My main objective with this project, as well as with the majority of my class assignments, is for each student to develop a deeper appreciation and set of values for the written word. With this understanding, they will ultimately see how theirs is a direct relationship to narrative form, visual interpretation, and effective, meaningful, and timeless solutions in visual communications.

What are the surprises that emerge from the project?

I am always surprised when I give this assignment because the outcome is never the same. Each student, while initially challenged and sometimes overwhelmed, ultimately finds their own way to connect with the narrative, as well as with a very personal part of themselves, and inevitably responds with a very unique solution. It is very fulfilling as an educator to be constantly surprised by your student's response to a class assignment.

You've given the project for some time, how has it changed?

The assignment has not changed over time, only my students' interpretations, approaches, and ultimate solutions.

Has it met your expectations?

I am extremely fortunate that most of the time this assignment (and more so, my students) have exceeded my expectations, mainly because time and time again they have challenged themselves with developing new ways of seeing, interpreting, and ultimately communicating the themes and messages of these narratives in unique and exciting ways that I had not considered previously.

← *On the Pulse of Morning* **book**

Student: Sarah Berends

GETTING RESULTS FROM A GREAT CLASS PROJECT

IT IS ONE THING TO DESIGN A GREAT PROJECT, another altogether to elicit meaningful results. One might assume that anything a teacher assigns to a student is going to be tackled with vigor and intelligence. Think again! Often a project will not be approached the way the teacher wants to see it done. After all, most students with full class loads are given so many projects they sometimes have to exercise triage—focusing on one or two at the expense of the others. So, another challenge for the teacher is to make certain that the student commits to the project. How this is accomplished may be as difficult as the riddle of the Sphinx or as easy as throwing a dog a bone. It comes down to presentation.

Of course, getting good grades—or the consequence of not getting them—is the single most compelling motivation for any student. But it is the teacher's job to promote the project with fervency and passion. As much as students will pick up on any hint that the project is just a routine assignment, they will also rise to the occasion of a special event. The trick is to make the class assignment into something so special that the students will have missed out on a unique experience by failing to perform at their most energetic level. If the presentation of the project is vigorous, it doesn't matter how routine (or even mundane) the problem is.

The result of any class project is to elicit class critiques that will stimulate and educate. If the project is presented in a convincing manner, the hoped-for end product—a valuable experience for student and teacher—will emerge.

WHAT TEACHERS WANT

STUDENTS WANT KNOWLEDGE, wisdom, experience, and ultimately jobs. Teachers want serious students who, in addition to absorbing all of the above and getting good jobs, will push design to its next level. How students respond to class projects often indicates exactly how successful they will be. ∎

The Student's Perspective

STUDENTS CRAVE CLASS PROJECTS that allow them to express their personalities while learning invaluable lessons about design. If the exercise is too easy, they cannot grow. Exemplary projects must vigorously challenge the students as they open their skill sets to brand new experiences. If, in the process, what they conceive adds luster to their portfolio, well, that is icing on the cake.

BENEFITING FROM A GREAT CLASS PROJECT

A PROJECT SHOULD TEST STUDENTS' technical and creative aptitudes, force them to think rapidly and strategically, and prepare them for future design challenges. So what else is new? What students want (and need) from an assignment may be subject to debate, but a survey of students from the School of Visual Arts revealed that they do agree when it comes to the principle attributes and goals of an exceptional project.

The first attribute of a great design project is that it promotes *critical thinking*. In being asked to grapple with the current culture's ideological, sociological, political, and historical contexts, students learn to come up with solutions to problems that most people believe are too big to tackle. Or they learn how to create and tell a compelling story visually without emotion or judgment. First and foremost, students value projects that demonstrate how to be a design problem solver; they also rank high assignments that address social issues. Some of the best briefs are conceptual—and demand acute thinking—such as designing a poster about a first creative memory, or repackaging something with no value into something of value. As one satisfied student put it, "A seemingly simple and overwhelmingly stupid assignment turned out to be one of underlying complexity and seriousness."

The second attribute of a successful project lies in the *faculty critiques*. A teacher's critical response exerts a huge influence on how students feel about and progress with their projects. Students consider the "crit" an essential part of the process. (Some students actually see being "ripped apart" in a crit as integral to their growth.) It is of immense help, especially early on, and enables the students to keep on track. They benefit from the experience and knowledge of the faculty, and when teachers understand what students are attempting to accomplish the end product improves. Students who want their work acknowledged by professionals especially

success and sometimes it's a huge disaster. But projects that force you to think strategically, creatively, and rapidly are the ones that help you prepare for the future."

Great class projects keep students on course and provide structure—and this is key. But they also encourage students to develop numerous skills that will serve them over time. Class projects are often cut and dry, but the best demand a modicum of individual interpretation. While being open ended has its drawbacks, problems that encourage divergence from the

While being open ended has its drawbacks, problems that encourage divergence from the standard are most valuable.

value one-on-one crits. Even late in the process, critiques can help refine and perfect an idea. "The faculty critiques shaped the direction of my idea—which was already quite developed," said another student. "However, I feel I was able to develop it through their expertise."

The third attribute of a great project is that it engenders *personal growth*. Students overwhelmingly agree that the best class projects are those that force them to develop in the most personal of ways. Creative challenges help students determine who they are as designers while inspiring them to think. Any class assignment through which the student reflects on how people are affected and touched by design provides substance for future work. Projects that lead students to understand the impact design can have on an intended audience make them feel that they are not just form givers but also content providers.

"A valuable class project is one which takes you through every possible emotion," said a student surveyed about projects in general. "You're excited, angry, indifferent. You question ethics and aesthetics. You plan things to go one way, but then something changes and you have to go back to the drawing board. Sometimes it's a

standard are most valuable. "I learned that the way you interpret the project brief," a student explained, "has a dramatic affect on how you do real-world work." Students also learn from their fellow classmates, especially how diverse everyone is—how they solve problems from different directions—and how important it is not to underestimate their talent and intelligence. Classmates can help set standards for pace and quality. "Seeing how different projects undergo the same steps proved inspiring," reported yet another student, "and allowed us to experiment together." Doing a project requires a lot of listening, to the brief, the teacher, and other students. But everyone has their own way of listening. As one student put it, "You can't listen to everybody, so you may as well listen to the opinions you instinctively agree with." And another said, "I learned to follow my gut and take an idea completely from thought to fruition."

Students routinely consider the worst class projects to be those that do not provide enough time. "When there is no time to even finish thinking about an idea, but you have to start executing it, like trying to design a website in one day," is typical of the complaints. Yet time constraints are part of the design process and understanding and adjusting to obstacles is part of accepting structure. Students are also unhappy with a class project when they feel ill equipped to complete it—but what better reason to engage a project than to find the right path? Still, students often equate a failed project with a lack of passion for the assignment in question. While there are always excuses for not doing well (and disinterest is not to be ignored), every project can be perceived as either an obstacle or an opportunity. Frequently, students say that good projects give them the confidence to come up with solutions to seemingly unsolvable problems or to leave their comfort zones and execute design in realms where the absence of total control is a requisite.

The measure of a successful project is not necessarily about the grade or the end result. "I'm not sure our end products were the best any of us has ever done," said a student, "but I think the important thing about the project was all the steps we had to go through along the way." For some students, the word "nightmare" precedes success: "It was a total nightmare, which is why I loved it. I had never work in the assigned medium before and I had nothing but problems. However, the end product turned out well, and since then I have used the process for other projects."

The answer to what makes for an interesting class project will always vary because every teacher and every student addresses a different set of agendas and priorities. Interesting and boring are two sides of the spectrum, but even in a single class they may overlap, depending on the students' needs. Students in the School of Visual Arts' MFA Designer as Author program weigh in with their perspectives.

Steven Haslip, Graduate Student

School of Visual Arts, New York, New York, USA

What was your most interesting class project?
The task was to make a visual presentation of a classmate's work, depicting their characteristics and qualities. We then had to design our own interpretation of ourselves.

Explain why this was the most interesting?
Designing for yourself is often the hardest task you can undertake. Only by looking at myself through someone else's lens was I able to begin to understand what I wanted to communicate to others. Acting as both client and designer gave me a greater understanding of the personal process of designing for yourself. I felt that with my classmates' often stunningly accurate analysis of my traits, I was better able to communicate my key qualities in spectacular ways.

What do you want to derive from a class project?
Distancing yourself from a project can be an effective method to understanding the message that you want to communicate. You need to ensure

that others see your vision. So looking through someone else's eyes is vital when designing for a client.

What is the most significant aspect of a class project?

I think that the creative process is often more important than the final product itself. Often, you learn far more through informal conversations with classmates than in the final critique. With this project, when working for a classmate, the project was kept a secret, which ensured that the final crit was an exciting and sometimes emotional affair.

How would you measure the success of a class project?

Although I feel that you learn most when you make the biggest mistakes, at the root of success was how closely the final work mirrored the individual it represented. At this point in the year, we knew each other's skills and characters to the point where the work resembled the person to an uncanny degree.

Have any class projects changed the way you think and work?

Yes, definitely. I think that the most enjoyable classes are where you question your existing habits and processes. Many classes have asked monumental questions, and there is nothing worse than having all of the answers. ■

Mariana Uchoa, Graduate Student

SCHOOL OF VISUAL ARTS, NEW YORK, NEW YORK, USA

The Guilt Trip

What was your most interesting class project?
Designing a pooper scooper.

Explain why this was the most interesting?
It was interesting to me to discover that the project was not about the object itself—there is no design problem there, people just use plastic or biodegradable bags to pick it up, no other product is necessary. The project was about the whole system, of scooping poop, and everything that it involves. Of course, we had to figure that out for ourselves, so the first week was a disaster—we all came to class with these terrible gadgets. Eventually we understood, and the results were very interesting.

What do you want to derive from a class project?
In this case, I really learned how to see the problem as a system, not as an object.

What is the most significant aspect of a class project?
All you can learn from the various stages—not necessarily the final result itself, but the whole process that leads to it.

How would you measure the success of a class project?
Success is when you see all students really getting what the project is about and finding out how to get the most out of it.

Have any class projects changed the way you think and work?
Absolutely. In another class, we were told to draw our "design process." It was hard at first to think about it, and realizing that I do have a step-by-step process that I follow when I work on a project. Then, we were shown alternatives to our processes. This is something that I am already incorporating in my process. ∎

Scott Suiter, Graduate Student

SCHOOL OF VISUAL ARTS, NEW YORK, NEW YORK

What was your most interesting class project?
I have done a lot of projects at SVA, but during an undergraduate branding class in UCLA's Design Media Arts program, various groups were asked to create a concept for a mobile device with no particular limitations in its functionality. Rather than jumping right into concepting, we were asked to do two weeks of field research. We had to carry around a six-inch piece of lumber throughout the day, and as we went through our routine we analyzed the situations in which a mobile device would be helpful. Beyond just carrying this piece of wood around throughout our daily activities, we were asked to visit airports, grocery stores, and sporting events, among other places. Through these experiences, gaps began to appear in which this mobile device could provide a solution to existing inefficiencies.

Explain why this was the most interesting?
It helped me look at my research in a whole new way. By carrying an inanimate object around, it was easy to freely associate the potential of its functionality. It helped me learn that research for a project can, and should, come from tangential sources.

What do you want to derive from a class project?
This project reconfirmed that research is the most important part of the design process. As I go through various projects, I am reminded to vary my methods of obtaining information on a subject.

What is the most significant aspect of a class project?
Trying out a new process. In an era when it is so easy to use the web for all research purposes, this project emphasized the importance of direct research tactics. By trying something new and somewhat uncomfortable at first, the limitations of my critical assessment were much more

relaxed. Similar to the cliché of a "blank canvas," this blank piece of wood was able to become anything my mind wanted it to be. It was only after all of the brainstorming did I have to go and find all of the logical means by which this product could function.

How would you measure the success of a class project?
The three-month timeframe of the class did not allow for material research, production, or a completed business model. Yet the success of the project was based on its potential viability. My group had developed a product to the point where we were able to get the panel of teachers and fellow students excited about its theoretical functionality. But the personal success of the project was the result of this new method of research providing me the opportunity to think in a new way.

Have any class projects changed the way you think and work?
I feel as though the education process is cumulative and that every class and learning experience has formed the way I think and work. ■

Irina Lee, Graduate Student

SCHOOL OF VISUAL ARTS, NEW YORK, NEW YORK, USA

What was your most interesting class project?

Street Signs for an Urban Design class. The teacher assigned the class to design street signs that were to be installed in public for real people to see. I created a real sign that urged moms to schedule mammograms. Thus the "My Mom / Your Mom" project was born.

Explain why this was the most interesting?

This project had a personal connection with something that meant a lot to me. My mom found out she had breast cancer that could have been detected early. Despite being a five-year-old tumor, she was fortunate that the cancer was Stage I. My mom wasn't getting annual mammograms. Had I known that, I would have urged her to get one and perhaps the tumor would have been found sooner.

My hope was to educate other sons and daughters that getting involved in their mother's health is easy and can make a real difference. Equally as interesting was what I learned about myself. I was taught how to overcome fear. My teacher taught me that great work will only come from your greatest loves and the greatest fears. He taught me how to grow balls and design from the heart, and not think—how to "just do what's in your heart and keep smiling." It's amazing how much power and meaning this project accumulated the less I feared and learned how to get out of my own way.

What do you want to derive from a class project?

I want a class project to make me scared. I need it to go beyond my safety zone and force me to suspend my feeling of security and disbelief. I want the class project to make a difference.

What is the most significant aspect of a class project?

It has to be personal. The project needs to touch something within me. I've found that when you speak to the few, the masses will follow.

How would you measure the success of a class project?

When the project takes on a life of its own and becomes bigger than you, you realize that you owe it to the project to keep working on it. You realize that it's no longer about going through the motions and completing the project. Instead, it becomes your obligation to keep going and to keep pushing the limits. That's what I think defines ultimate success.

Have any class projects changed the way you think and work?

Every project I completed for Urban Design taught me how to unlearn everything I ever thought about design. Prior to taking this class, I was so focused on "design" and being spiffy. Looking back, I think I was just scared. My teacher taught me to see that design is empty if it's not personal. He taught me how to be fearless and how to take huge risks. If your work doesn't resonate or grab something from your inside, then what's the point? Before, I was really concerned with the creative brief, the client's or teacher's opinion, the project parameters and everything else except what was in my heart. When you can honestly be happy with your work, nothing else matters. Everything I do now is for myself, for my mom, for the people that I love the most. I will now do what's in my heart and keep smiling. ∎

WHAT STUDENTS WANT

ULTIMATELY, STUDENTS MAY ENTER a project with a healthy amount of skepticism, and if it piques their interest, they leave with desired results. Success and failure are not necessarily mutually exclusive. The student who gets a high grade for a job well done and the one who gets a mediocre grade but learns more than when the project began may derive the very same satisfaction. ∎

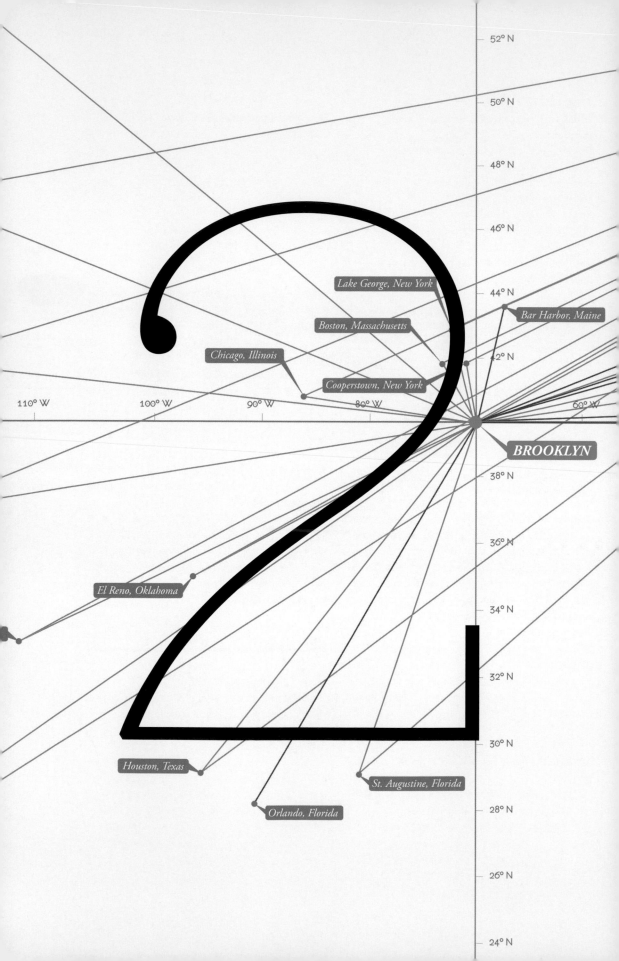

Section 2

The Projects

WE ASKED OVER FIFTY TEACHERS from art and design schools and programs around the world to present their most interesting or challenging class projects. The results are varied, though social consciousness is a common yet not exclusive thread.

We asked the teachers to provide a project goal, objective, and outcome. While most offered the first two, sometimes the objective and outcome were one and the same. We asked the students to provide a title and a statement of purpose. Here, consistency falls short. Most students could articulate their goal, but some could not. Many had titles, but some projects were not individual enough to merit a separate title. Ultimately, the work speaks for itself in the context of the fundamental problem, but some are distinct because they transcend the problem.

What can we learn from these projects? Aside from seeking fluency and expertise, the teachers are attempting to instill a sense of wonder in their students, and the students are trying to use their design talents to convey narratives as well as to explore forms that they will use later in their careers.

Helvetica Nation

Maryland Institute College of Art

BALTIMORE, MARYLAND, U.S.A.

Class: Graphic Design II
Level: Sophomore
Senior Faculty Member: Ellen Lupton
Duration of Project: Two Weeks

PROJECT BRIEF
Create a set of icons using the typeface Helvetica Bold. Use the knife tool in Illustrator to cut letters into pieces. Do not change the letters' scale and do not skew or distort them or fill in the counters.

Do not edit or change the underlying path of the letters. You can copy and reuse parts of the letters. Make eight icons. Your icons can represent anything: men, women, children, aliens, athletes, robots, doggies, useful objects, abstract ideas, and so on. Your icons should work together as a system (similar scale, level of detail, etc).

PROJECT GOAL
Working with constraints; conveying ideas through minimal means; mastering Adobe Illustrator tools.

↑ Student: Alex Roultette

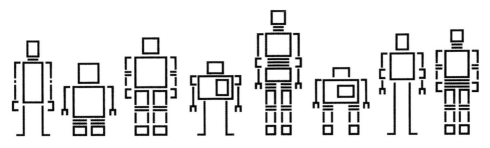

↑ Student: Colin Ford

↑ Student: David Colson

↑ Student: Yu Chen

↑ Student: Christine Ricks

↑ Student: Allie Kanik

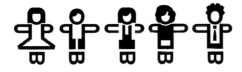

↑ Student: Arda Erdogan

↑ Student: Julia Kostreva

VCUQatar 10th Anniversary Publication

Virginia Commonwealth University, School of the Arts in Qatar

DOHA, QATA

Class: Graphic Design II
Level: Sophomore
Faculty: Senior Pornprapha Phatanateacha
and Law Alsobrook
Duration of Project: Six Weeks

PROJECT BRIEF

Typography is the lifeblood of graphic design. The aim of this project is to help develop an understanding of type and its use as a larger body of text in relationship to publication design, usability, clients, and content manifestation for an audience. This project further extends the student's chance to experiment with typographic function, organization, and aesthetics. To begin, the student will be designing both the concept and the specs for the VCUQatar 10th anniversary publication. This project will be a longer, more involved process than previous projects, but will continue with many of the same issues: hierarchy, audience, rhythm, pacing, sequence, type choice and use, etc. The systems become more involved, but they also help to set limitations. Breaking the rules makes for interest.

PROJECT GOAL

This project was designed to help students recognize and apply the basic knowledge they have acquired during their sophomore year and the first semester of their junior year. The holistic nature of this project allowed students to design a concept for an actual project with real clients, an audience, and content. The strategic planning of the project enabled students to experience various stages of the design process of a large publication. The project kicked off with the clients—in this case, the dean and associate dean of VCUQatar—explaining their goal and vision enabling the students to develop an understanding of the project through questions and answers, much like a typical initial design phase. To encourage teamwork among the students, the class was divided into groups, with each member of the group supplying different skills. Following the question-and-answer session, the student teams developed five different project briefs and proposals. As a result, students could see the generation of various design permutations and directions. Upon completion of this phase, the student teams were split and individual students were encouraged to implement the concept based on their group's design direction. Ultimately, students were required to submit a specification manual of the final design with guidelines for typographic treatment, color palette, image usage, art direction for photographs, materials, etc. Samples of the actual spreads, as well as the design manual, were presented to the clients and juried for final selection.

PROJECT OUTCOME

Among the expressed outcomes for the project, the students were exposed to the process of publication design in as close to a real-world scenario as possible, from interactions with clients to design team ideation, and ultimately to individual design implementation. As part of the class, many prepress issues were also covered in order that students begin to underst and the translation of their ideas into practical and applicable design solutions for the printed page. In the end, students garnered invaluable experience, from both a design and production aspect, of how large bodies of text go from a mass of words to the harmonious composition of text, image, color, and concept on the printed page.

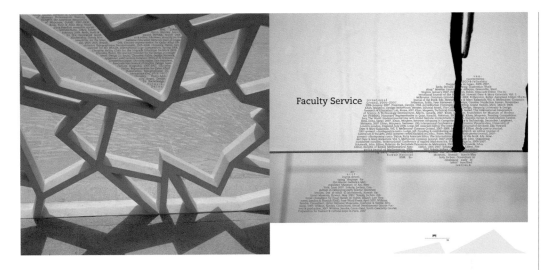

↑ Student: Sahar Mari; Junior designer: Zeina Said Hamady; Interns: Rana Selo, Fatma Al Mansouri; Photographer: Markus Elblaus

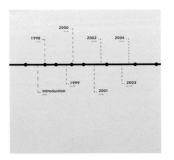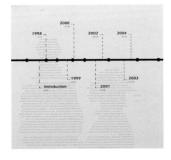

↑ Student: Sahar Mari

Junior designer: Zeina Said Hamady

Interns: Rana Selo, Fatma Al Mansouri

Photographer: Markus Elblaus

The group I was a part of felt that the idea of leaving a mark successfully embodied a decade of design, not only in VCUQatar but also in the surrounding communities and regions influenced by its progress. As a double major in graphic design and fashion design, I decided to apply the basic tools that link my two areas of study throughout the publication: carbon tracing paper and stencils. By experimenting with these tools, it soon became clear that the nature of the guiding concept suggested an interactive design. The principle of "leaving a mark" is literally inscribed on the pages of this publication by featuring an original piece or work followed by its impact—depicted as a shadow traced on the subsequent pages. This technique allowed the work to leave its own, unique impression while still retaining parts of its original features. The inspiration for this technique evolved out of the structure of our own VCUQatar education; stencils symbolize our education in design theory while the notion of leaving a mark represents our instruction in practical application.

↓ Student: Fatma Al Mansouri

We chose active, bright colors to grab the attention of the reader and step away from the colors that are traditionally used in publications issued by VCUQatar: yellow for warmth and hope, but also as it relates to our traditions and culture; blue to symbolize water, but our research showed that it also implies a feeling of youth and energy; green for a classic color that is also zestful, luscious, juicy, and plentiful and gives a feeling of nature; and, lastly, pink as a passionate color that is full of energy and at the same time attention getting. My main goal was to find a sans serif typeface to make the publication easy to read. I was also looking for one that has a variety of styles and weights so it can be used as display, title, or running text. Myriad met the qualifications because it is a classic typeface with rounded counter forms that give a feeling of a handwritten script. On the other hand, I choose Boutros Ads Pro for the Arabic typeface. It has sharper edges—something we intended, to create a contrast between the Arabic and English typefaces. I included patterns as design elements to show the cultural influence this area of the world has on the publication. I placed these patterns on transparent paper to illustrate the idea that culture and design influence each other. I chose a collection of images that suggest spontaneous, cheerful, and active life, all the while combining them with the culture they represent, the Middle East. Most images document the process of students' work, including each major and the freshmen foundation year. Cropping and odd angles emphasize different cultures and different points of view.

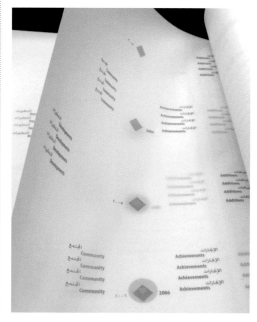

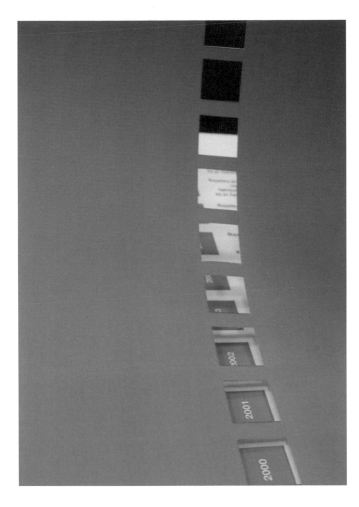

↑ Student: Ruda Ismail Zainal
Additional credits: Zeina Said Hamady;
junior designer; Rana Selo and Fatma Al Mansouri,
interns, and Markus Elblaus, photographer

I used Helvetica Neue in different sizes in the publication. It is a clean and static typeface, which gave me the freedom to play with it using different techniques. The bright colors are to catch the attention of the audience. These colors were taken from elements in the environment such as dunes, water, sunsets, and trees (yellow, blue, purple, and green). These colors let the audience experience the history of Qatar and VCUQatar. Each chapter owned one color to help the viewer distinguish between topics. Our main concept is that of "leaving a mark." I tried to show how VCUQatar leaves indelible marks in the lives of its students. This was the equation I used: knowledge + culture = many possibilities. I developed this concept by representing knowledge and culture through simple shapes, which change according to the impact knowledge and culture have on each other, creating endless possibilities. I used diecuts to represent the impact the past has on our future. These cuts left shadows on the next page, and when the page is flipped, part of the past page is emerging with the next page, similar to reality.

Cradle to Grave

London College of Communication

LONDON, UK

Class: Diploma in Professional Studies
Level: First Year
Faculty: Sarah Temple
Duration of Project: One Semester

PROJECT BRIEF

Select a durable household product, like a hair dryer, dishwasher, or anything that's used a lot, and research and analyze it. Then design a visual representation of its lifetime use of material resources from cradle to grave. You are required to create a visual in a medium that can be accessible and useable for consumers to see prior to purchase of these products. (This project was part of the D&AD live briefs.)

PROJECT GOAL

The target audience was to be the general public, especially those who believe it important to know about a product's ecological status before buying it. It would be significant to consider our extensive global-warming issues and the urgency of beginning to think differently and be more aware of our spending and waste levels of energy. Much wasted matter is invisible, and as designers, we should highlight this visually and make it simple for everyone to understand the environmental impact of their purchases.

← Environmental Labeling

Student: Laura Harvey

Through research, I discovered six common life-cycle stages that a given product goes through. I chose to develop the six stages into a labeling system that details the environmental impact of a product at each stage in its life cycle. I illustrated the labeling system by developing a series of icons to represent each stage. As well, I used color coding, stage titles, and a percentage of the environmental values of each stage to allow for instant recognition and more in-depth information. This system could work on a whole range of durable products.

**← Tree/Chair:
How Comfortably Do
You Sit on This Issue?**

Student: Neil Coward

I wanted to show the life of a wooden product (in my case, a chair), from beginning to end, in a very simple and visual way. I considered the sustainability of an organization such as IKEA, and wondered whether or not they provide us with good products. By pulling the wood out of the tree at the start, I was attempting to symbolize the source of wood. When wood is recycled, it gets turned into sawdust (one of the main recycling methods), which is then used to create paper. I deliberately chose to portray the process in a fun way for young people to understand and to broaden their knowledge of buying wood products.

← Green Gaming

Student: Himali Patel

Green Gaming is a maze designed to show how a mobile phone is constructed through the materials and manufacturing processes. The aim of the game is to collect all the phone parts in order to get maximum points and important information about each part. The game also informs the player of the consequences various parts have for the environment if not disposed of properly.

LOCATION: to be used at a supermarket checkout conveyor belt.

← What Goes Around, Comes Around

Student: Tom Prendergast

I created a moving panel on the grocery store checkout conveyor, so that consumers can see what happens to plastic bags once they are disposed of. I designed three graphic panels that would recycle constantly, reminding the queuing customers to avoid taking plastic bags unnecessarily.

↓ Biro Bleed

Student: Cavella Pottinger

The biro pen is small and generic, but not really considered to cause an environmental impact. I came up with my concept experimenting with inks as material, inspired by ink stains on pockets when a biro bleeds,. I filled thirty-six cups with ink and color-coded the life cycles of raw material (black ink), production (blue), usage (green), and end of life (red). The level of ink in each cup was then equivalent to the hierarchy of information printed on it. I created an extremely long pull-out book for the consumer.

Cradle to Grave - Lifetime Use of Resources of a Tumble Dryer

1. The materials used to construct 1 tumble dryer have traveled over 50000 km, this is equivalent to traveling 4 times around the world.

3. Iron from Australia — 16998 km

4. Steel from China — 9462 km

5. Aluminium from Jamaica — 1641 km

6. Copper from USA — 1844 km

7. Polyolefins from UK — 106 km

8. PVC from USA — 7944 km

9. The journey of 50000 km uses 183734 liters of fuel. This is equivalent to filling 2000 Bath tubs.

10. X 2000

11. 183734 liters of fuel emits over 3 tones of CO_2

13. Manufacturing 1 tumble dryer wastes 16 times its weight in materials.

15. In the UK 1 in 4 households own a tumble dryer.

17. The energy used to run a tumble dryer for a year, is the equivalent needed to light 300 households for a year.

18. = 300 X

19. A tumble dryer uses 4 times as much energy then a washing machine.

21. Over 15160 lbs of CO_2 are emitted in the life cycle of 1 tumble dryer.

22. 15160 lbs

23. In the UK household products are responsible for 1/3 of the nations CO_2 emissions.

24. CO_2

25. If every family in the UK hung out 1 wash per week, this would reduce CO_2 emission by 515000 tones.

27. Instead of recycling materials from existing tumble dryers, new machines are produced using more natural resources.

29. At the end of a tumble dryers life, 5 out of 7 machines end up in landfill.

↑ Washing Line Installation

Student: Seral Mustafa

My installation aimed to make the public aware of the heavy cost in energy and materials required to run tumble dryers. They are costly, inefficient to run, and complex to produce. The Weee Directive calls upon all producers of electrical equipment to take legal responsibility for their disposal. My installation attempted to encourage the public to use wind power to dry their washing.

Visual Identity for the 25th Biennial of Graphic Arts in Ljubljana

University of Ljubljana Academy of Fine Arts and Design

LJUBLJANA, SLOVENIA

Class: Typography 3
Level: Third Year
Faculty: Eduard Cehovin
Duration of Project: Two Semesters

PROJECT GOAL

Students should focus on the use of the letter and text as the fundamental visual and communication tools in connection with other pictorial elements. The basic instructions: to create comprehensive solutions instead of partial ones. This way the solutions would highlight how well the students grasped the conceptual orientation toward typography assignments, employing all the experience and knowledge gained at other subjects. The curators of the graphic arts biennial provided detailed descriptions of content and formal trends in the modern art graphics, which gave the students a better insight into modern graphic practice as a reproduction method. The final result of the work in both semesters reflected the maturity of students in understanding modern conceptual typographical solutions.

↑ Student: Luka Mancini

↑ Student: Matjaz Cuk

↑ Student: Spela Kasal

↑ Student: Irena Ocepek

On Trial

The Arts Institute at Bournemouth

POOLE, DORSET, UK

Class: B.A. (Honors) Graphic Design Unit: Locating Contemporary Practice
Level: First Year
Faculty: Kirsten Hardie
Duration: Six Weeks

PROJECT BRIEF

On Trial is a teaching strategy used to facilitate and promote creativity in learning. Graphic design students explore and interrogate problems relating to their specialization. On Trial embraces student-centered, experiential, problem-based learning through a "teaching-with-your-mouth-shut" approach (Finkel, 2000). Using this approach forces students to question, defend, and judge a problem.

On Trial harnesses popular culture and the seductive qualities of the courtroom to help students engage with tough academic issues and wider ethical concerns. Students learn the protocols and contexts of law through the popular media and bring such understandings into the classroom without formal teaching. The formal scenario enhances communication skills, critical analysis, group work, and research.

PROJECT ACTIVITIES

This approach comprises two integrated components: a written essay and a group role-playing event. Both activities focus upon the same theme, but the role playing is not assessed. The group event is specifically staged two weeks before the essay deadline so that students may prepare, develop, test, and review their research, ideas, and examples before completing their assessed individual essay.

ACTIVITY 1: ON TRIAL: "FIRST THINGS FIRST" MANIFESTO

Write an essay of two thousand words that addresses the "First Things First" 2000 design manifesto.

Develop an argument that either supports or contests the claims/ethos of the 1964 and 2000 manifestos. Discuss your viewpoint and substantiate this with relevant examples, facts, and the views of others. Relate your discussion to the critical consideration of the work of a contemporary designer/agency or a specific area of design work. Refer to historical examples as appropriate. Ultimately, consider whether it is appropriate and acceptable for contemporary graphic designers to work in, and for, specific commercial contexts.

Select your focus and approach carefully, research and write the essay in relation to the set brief and compile your bibliography. (The essay must follow academic conventions and be accompanied by a bibliography.) Ensure that your discussion applies to appropriate contemporary design examples and theoretical ideas and texts.

ACTIVITY 2: ON TRIAL

To inform and support your written assignment and to develop your wider professional awareness and understanding of your subject specialism, you are required to work in a creative group role-play activity.

Through group work, you will consider and test key issues, approaches, and examples relating to the First Things First manifesto to judge whether the manifesto is relevant, viable, appropriate, and acceptable in the context of contemporary graphic design. You will work in roles relevant to a courtroom scenario:

- Prosecution Team
- Defense Team
- 1 Twelve-person Jury, including foreperson
- Witnesses—for defense and prosecution
- Three Judges
- Note Takers
- Gallery
- Three Ushers—bring witnesses to stand and responsible for jury
- Court Clerk
- Three Clerks—one for each judge
- Journalists/Press Team
- Film Crew
- Photographers

This activity requires each member of the course to select a key role from the list above. Then, using research undertaken to date for the related written assignment, as well as further research, you will develop materials to inform and support your role accordingly.

By examining communication styles and techniques, we can learn to communicate more effectively verbally and nonverbally (body language). To help you in your awareness and understanding of courtroom communication protocols and performance, you are encouraged to select and critically view at least one film from the following list and consider these scenarios and develop and apply these skills accordingly:

- Taking a claim, presenting a case
- Developing a convincing argument
- Supporting and substantiating an argument with evidence
- Questioning (various methods)
- Critically analyzing and evaluating a case presented
- Arguing a case, defending an argument, and deflecting questions
- Appealing to an audience
- Listening to a presentation to extract vital information

To Kill a Mockingbird
The Verdict
Twelve Angry Men
A Few Good Men
The Client
Anatomy of a Murder
The Pelican Brief
High Crimes
A Civil Action
Rules of Engagement
The Caine Mutiny
King Rat
Erin Brockovitch
A Soldier's Story
Witness for the Prosecution
Presumed Innocent
The Young Philadelphians
Runaway Jury
Matter of Life and Death
Breaker Morant
Amistad

↑ **2006 class in court**

All photos by Sam Tylor and Adam Bowen

↑ Jenny South, 2008 defense team

↑ 2008 judges

↑ Lucy Bywater and Rob Wilson, 2008 judges

↑ 2006 prosecution team

Student: Simon Burch (witness), 2007
The trial based on the "First Things First" manifesto was a great insight into a side of graphics that large companies and lower education courses don't teach. There were strong arguments from each side.

Student: Harry Smith (judge), 2008
As a judge in the proceedings, it was fascinating to watch the battle between the two sides arguing the feasibility of the manifesto. Hearing evidence for and against the manifesto from key witnesses, like original author Ken Garland, not only placed the manifesto into context, but also allowed us, as the next generation of designers, to question and understand our role in the manifesto's future.

Student: Keir Cooper (defense), 2006
This was a great intellectual exercise, and draining in a satisfying way.

Student: Lindsay Noble (prosecution), 2006
The three-hour trial was pretty intense. It was a mix of hard work and big fun. Taking part in such an event should be mandatory. I learned a lot.

Student: Ashley May (defense), 2005
The purpose of the debate scenario is not to indoctrinate students toward a career of anti-consumerism, nor to be the route to a definitive solution; if this were the case, we'd be rich and be able to sleep soundly at night. It engages all participants and is a catalyzing, beneficial debate. My entire final year was devoted to projects and assignments concerning the nature of design, the designer's responsibility in terms of output, and how a designer might follow a career path that would allow later reflection without horrible guilt at the negative impact made on society, culture, or the environment.

Student: Carla Hicks, 2008
It was an inspirational experience to work with the creator of the original "First Things First" manifesto, Ken Garland, gaining an insight into his knowledge and experience.

Student: Jonathan Oldaker, 2008
It was great to see individuals' passions coming out in the court case scenario. It put people on the spot and created elements of seriousness and tension. It also made it fun, enjoyable, and, in some cases, amusing.

Student: Dan Rowland, 2008
Having the opportunity to role-play a court case not only drew us closer together as a group, it also encouraged us to research the notion of quotation in a degree of detail that pushed us to excel in order to succeed. Never before have I left a room with so much knowledge.

Product Identity

Alberta College of Art and Design

CALGARY, ALBERTA, CANADA

Class: Advanced Graphic Design I —
Product Identity
Level: Fourth Year
Faculty: Rik Zak
Duration of Project: One Semester

PROJECT BRIEF

Create an identity for a hypothetical product. If your product is based on an existing consumer product, target a new market segment and make appropriate modifications to the product.

Identify your audience and develop an understanding of their needs. Use these insights to shape your design decisions.

Analyze and evaluate the product and its competitive context.

Identify the target consumer, their needs, and their relationship to the product in a manner that will allow you to find them. If you can find them, you can reach them easily: This means that your audience has already established high-quality hubs, communication networks, etc. (If members of your target audience are dog owners, for example, then you can find them through vets, pet stores, dog parks, dog magazines, groomers, kennels, web zines, dog shows, and dog trainers.)

Define the core idea behind your product. (A target + a problem = the core idea or product niche.)

Identify the key problem(s) your product addresses: Understanding your consumers' problem is how you reach them emotionally. Your ability to articulate the pain, needs, problems, and desires of your prospects is the centerpiece to how much they will trust you, your ability to come up with irresistible offers and messages, and whether or not you can even get their attention in the first place. Techniques and tactics are not the heart of great marketing.

Translate the core product idea into a powerful and memorable product identity by developing and executing the key product identity elements such as product name, logo, and packaging.

PROJECT GOAL

- Demonstrate advanced research skills.
- Demonstrate the ability to compile, organize, and edit data.
- Explore the relationship of brand development to product.
- Develop an understanding of a target audience.
- Develop an effective design strategy related to consumer needs.
- Demonstrate the ability to develop a design strategy and create an integrated product-identity program.

PROJECT OUTCOME

- Produce an identity program that includes a minimum of the following components:
- Logo/word mark
- Package design
- Promotion material and/or point-of-purchase environment
- Booklet that documents your process
- The presentation must include a design brief that outlines product evaluation, consumer evaluation, and objectives and strategy.

↑ Little Boy Identity

Student: Justin Tan

I wanted to take a line of retro Japanese sneakers and make it a counterculture street product. I created an identity based on Japanese post-apocalyptic film language, World War II references, and Japanese *kawaii* culture. The logo contrasts the seriousness of the expression "little boy" with a smiling Buddha, referencing Japanese culture in a tongue-in-cheek manner. The use of "Engrish" gives the impression that the product is intended for the Japanese and has simply been imported.

→ Apostle Identity

Student: Rachel Rivera
Illustrations: Brennan Kelly

Create longboards for sophisticated indie boarders that reflect their attitudes and alternative lifestyles. Rebrand Arbor's series of elite carver-style decks featuring custom artwork by young contemporary artists.

The objective is to cast a different light on the longboarding lifestyle, veering away from the thrasher or punk aesthetic, to something more enlightened and philosophical.

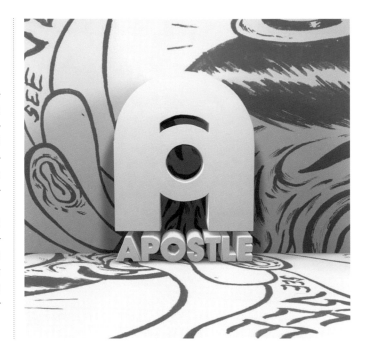

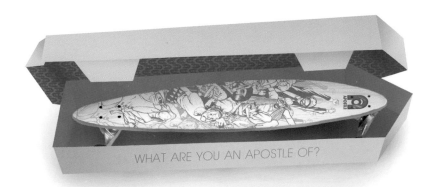

← Soop Toys Wordmark and Logo

Student: Matt Luckhurst

Soop Toys are based on a character I created in a paintng called Johnny Don't Smoke in the House, a character from a painting I did that was then sculpted by Sam Longbotham. Soop was created to reflect the sense of humor in the paintings and the nostalgic qualities of soup and toys. This strategy is also reflected in the logo and labeling, both through color and type. The vinyl toy market targets older collectors, who appreciate art but also want to recapture a part of their childhood, so I believe the overall design strategy for Soop is a strong one.

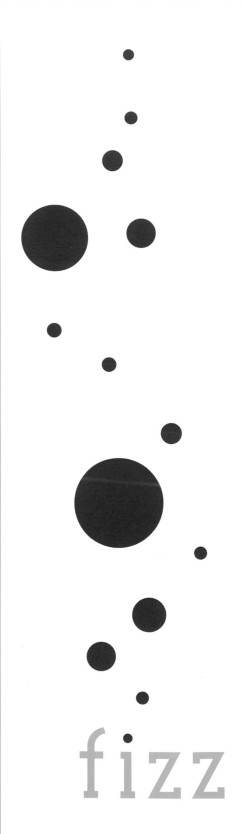

↑ Fizz Logo

Student: Josh Smith

The objective was to create a memorable identity for a modern soda shop that serves organic, natural soda to a young urban clientele (approximately 20 to 35 years of age). The strategy was to try to create a modern, clean look in the brand, but give it some unexpected twists (like the product concept itself). Bright color and an unexpected vertical format make the logo stand out among others without being gimmicky or overcomplicated.

← **Pinkeye Identity**

Student: Katherine Kinasewich

My objective was to take a collection of vintage 1980s eyewear and reintroduce it as a current street product using an identity based on old-school hiphop language and electronica culture, with the concept of contaminated eyesight. Each letter of the logo is designed with braille. In most cases, the braille must be embossed to further emphasize the problem at hand.

08 catalogue photoshoot: Motel

start slideshow   collection   locations   order   history

Locale

American University of Sharjah, School of Architecture and Design

SHARJAH, EMIRATE OF SHARJAH, UNITED ARAB EMIRATES

Class: Senior Design Studio
Level: Fourth Year
Faculty: Amir Berbic, Roderick Grant, and Shoaib Nabi
Duration of Project: Six Weeks

PROJECT BRIEF

In this project, students responded to a specific outdoor site. It began as a process of experiencing, through as many senses as possible, an assigned location. Encouraged to employ a variety of methods and media for documenting and generating form, students were expected to both engage the site and allow it to affect them by their participation in, or observation of, its form. The studio critique was a visual and verbal review of their experienced environment through images, footage, recordings, and found objects. The processes that evolved out of such discussion began to reflect each student's unique interpretation of what is important to the development of an identity of place.

PROJECT GOAL

The idea of local identity has become ubiquitous; it has been reduced, simplified, and, in some respects, made obsolete by the reach of consistent global marketing. What might it mean to begin the process of identity design without the need to compete on a global scale? The primary objective of this project is to develop strategies, processes, and forms that avoid convention and embrace a more responsive and expressive notion of what an identity could be in today's visual culture.

PROJECT OUTCOME

The outcomes of this project are defined by three distinct formats: an A5 book, an A1 poster, and a time-based short. The results were as var-

ied as the students participating in the studio; however, certain central themes and motivations became clear across both print- and time-based work. The inconsistency of each site in Sharjah and neighboring Dubai's constantly evolving infrastructure gave students the challenge of attempting to fix their sites in time. The process of refinement involved the identification of behaviors and activities within a location. In place of trying to fix a static identity, students embraced constant change as an aspect of identity itself. While the possible range of forms seemed infinite, the interaction of specific forms and specific behaviors allowed students to assess their progress through finite strategies.

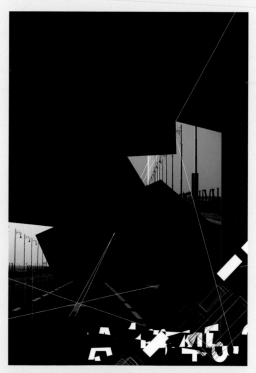

↑ Student: Maria Al Daoudi

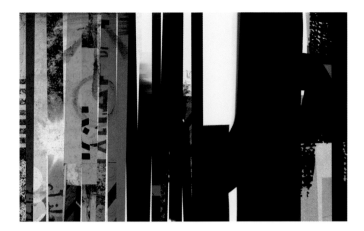

← Student: Sarah Al Kathem

When visiting King Faisal Street, the effect of light on the different sides inspired this design.

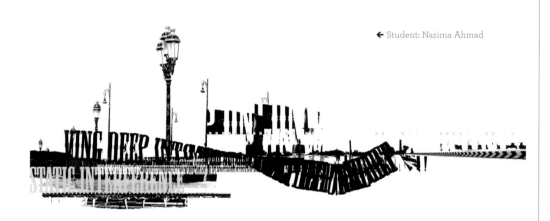

← Student: Nazima Ahmad

← Student: Faris Sarrar

↓ Student: Asraa Zayed

↓ Student: Raed Skaik

My project is a journey through Dubai's Al Diyafah Road, witnessed through form and color—a rhythmic experience that reflects the site's varied personality. I attempt to record the dynamic interplay of elements in the space.

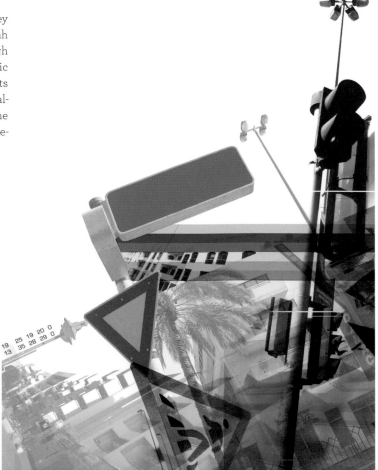

↑ Student: Fatma Alken

Spending days on King Faisal Road, watching people, machines, traffic, the construction of a bridge, and construction signage, I realized this is a place of constant and instant change; a place full of rawness, residue, and fragmentation.

→ Student: Farnoosh Rezapour

The various identities could be seen as distinguishing characteristics.

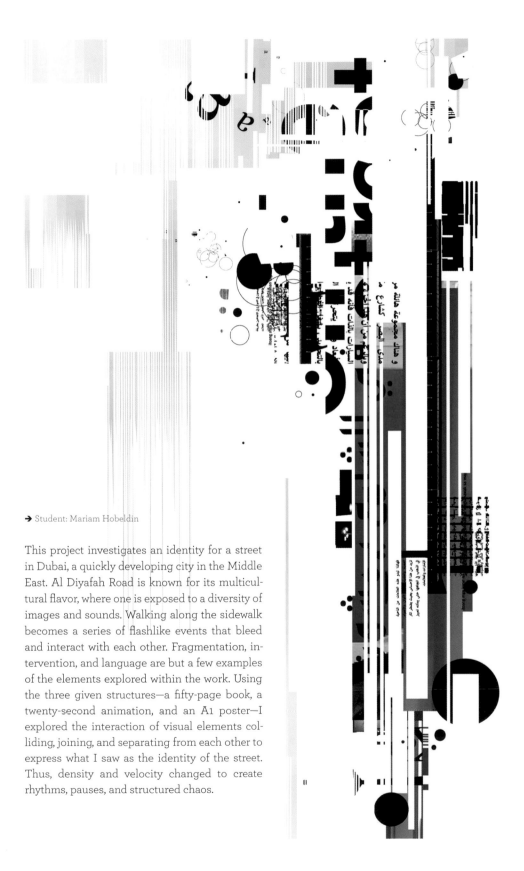

→ Student: Mariam Hobeldin

This project investigates an identity for a street in Dubai, a quickly developing city in the Middle East. Al Diyafah Road is known for its multicultural flavor, where one is exposed to a diversity of images and sounds. Walking along the sidewalk becomes a series of flashlike events that bleed and interact with each other. Fragmentation, intervention, and language are but a few examples of the elements explored within the work. Using the three given structures—a fifty-page book, a twenty-second animation, and an A1 poster—I explored the interaction of visual elements colliding, joining, and separating from each other to express what I saw as the identity of the street. Thus, density and velocity changed to create rhythms, pauses, and structured chaos.

Turning Data into Information

Art Center College of Design

PASADENA, CALIFORNIA, USA

Class: Information Design
Level: Third Year
Faculty: Sean Donahue
Duration of Project: Nine Weeks

PROJECT BRIEF

This project is preceded by several exercises that introduce the students to the concepts of information design. It is the core project for the class and the primary vehicle for presenting information design within the context of a viewing community.

To begin your project you will select one of the following as a starting point: a topical issue, a community, or a space or place.

Using the strategies of discovery introduced in your Art of Research class, educate yourself about the unique characteristics of your starting point. You will then present what you've discovered to the class next week as a graphic response. Over the following two weeks, you will move to one of the other starting points and do the same until you've covered all three areas.

Once this process is completed, you will present a graphic proposal that shares the relevant data sets of your issue, the community to which this is relevant (either positively or negatively), and the space and place you feel they would be best reached. This proposal should include a minimum of three different data sets and sources.

PROJECT GOAL

In an effort to move students away from producing work based on their preconceptions of what information design is—the result of which is too often a student mastering how to craft formats and not communication—the class rejects format-based assignment-control devices. Instead, the class places emphasis on qualities of content and

intent, which, in this case, is dealing with a quantity, depth, and breadth of content and turning data into information. This emphasizes a conversation about a range of possible design directions with which to achieve this goal and provides students with the framework to articulate their design decisions based on how they used the elements of design to achieve a particular intent.

PROJECT OUTCOME

Outcomes vary: Since the students are not given a format as the project-control device or a design restriction, and instead are asked to recognize the type of content and intent, they each develop a design approach and visual language unique to the situation they have identified and the communication they are attempting to facilitate. Work is assessed on how they have handled quantities, depths, and breadths of data and how their design has, through an awareness of context, enabled viewers to translate data into information.

↑ **A Global Warning**

Student: Gavin Alaoen

Models: Pei-Jeane Chen, Daniel Chang, and Ken Quemuel

These images link the causes of skin cancer with the steady increase of global warming.

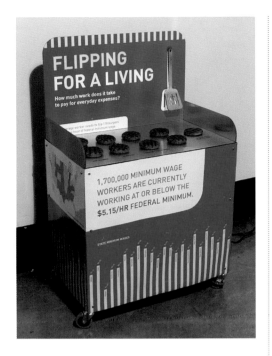

← Flipping for a Living

Student: Owen Gee

This project was conceived as a way to engage the viewer with the topic of minimum wage. By using design to deliver an experience as well as information, it provided a more tactile and personal encounter. Audio clips of burger grills and a smoke machine mimicked an actual fast-food job. The information could be found by interacting with—physically flipping—each burger. Each burger represented some basic living necessity in relation to how many burgers one would need to flip to obtain it. The cart ended up in a student gallery where it was used frequently until it was disassembled.

→ You Stink!

Student: Aaron Bjork

My main premise was to encourage my fellow schoolmates not to smoke by making fun of them. After insulting them for various adverse effects that smoking has on the body, the signs inform the readers with scientific data supporting the insult. Once completed, the signs were placed around campus in prime smoking locations.

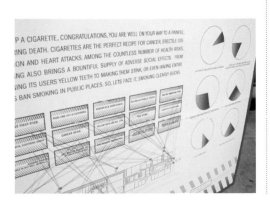

U.S. Arms Recipients in the Developing World

Student: Sean Starkweather

Each year, the United States exports billions of dollars in arms to developing countries around the world, many of which are undemocratic with poor human rights records. My goal was to present this comparative data in a manner that conveyed the immense scale of this spending. After being cleared to use a portion of the campus building façade, I had to find a relatively in-expensive way to construct this very short-lived installation. Many of the design decisions were informed by this constraint and by the strong grid created by the building windows and frame-work. Throughout the entire class, I was intro-duced to methods of research that deepened my understanding of the subject and greatly influenced the final form of the project. It was

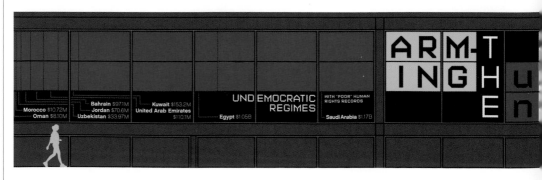

my first experience creating such a site-specific design. I spent much of the design process exploring potential "canvases" around the campus that would most effectively present the intended message. I am grateful I had the opportunity to create work of such a large scale.

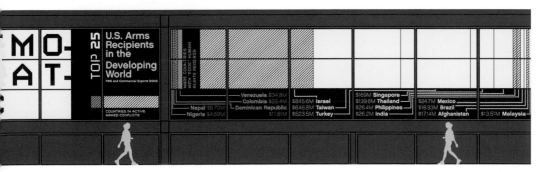

Sacral Design

Berlin University of the Arts

BERLIN, GERMANY

Class: Digital Media Design
Level: Junior and Senior
Faculty: Jussi Ängeslevä and Joachim Sauter
Duration of Project: One Semester

PROJECT BRIEF
Sacral objects have extremely varied uses and meanings in world religions. They have evolved over time to their strictly defined present-day forms. The development of sacral objects has been largely left to craftsmen, with little critical exposition by designers. Hence, the results are often ornamental adaptations of legacy objects that reflect a period of time. A more critical eye on the function of different religious objects is a timely topic for media designers to engage with beyond a pure artisanship.

PROJECT GOAL
In teaching digital media, technology can often take the upper hand in dictating what gets designed and with what means. The project goal was to start from the other extreme, to focus on meaning, history, and societal perspectives. The goal was to employ principles of digital media in rethinking religious objects, to try to distill the essence of what *digitality* means—especially today, where technology has yielded almost religious proportions.

PROJECT OUTCOME
The working prototypes and artifacts have been exhibited in several galleries and shows and have appeared in different publications, stirring public discussions on the subject.

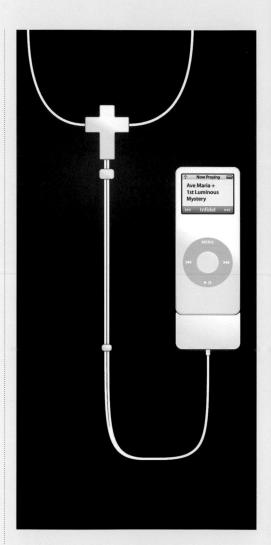

↑ iRosary
Student: Tino Dobra

For years, the rosary prayer has been losing its significance in folk piety because this kind of prayer fails to appeal to younger people due to its monotonous nature. Put a rosary interface on an iPod, and you have a whole new audience.

→ iRauch

Student: Felix Hardmood Beck

The Catholic Church uses the media to send a valid benediction "Urbi et Orbi" around the world. iRauch allows absentees to be at the place of the happening.

→ Way of the Cross

Student: Jens Wunderling

This is a contemporary symbolic reconstruction of the Passion of Christ in the form of a sound installation: When approaching one of the fourteen stations of the traditional Way of the Cross, audio files are played on an MP3 player hidden in the wooden cross. News articles—for example, about socially deprived people or help in time of need—give a modern interpretation of the stations.

↑ Crucifixion

Student: Markus Kison

The cross has become an abstract symbol, while the events at the place of the crucifixion tend to be forgotten. The installation intended for the side altar of a church, tells these stories.

↑ Living Torah

Student: Jan Lindenberg

A reactive membrane is the communicating element between the Torah scroll and its reader. Between the readings, the membrane's ornaments spread dynamically over the Torah and separates the holy from the profane.

New Identity for the Academy of Fine Arts of Bologna

Academy of Fine Arts of Bologna

BOLOGNA, ITALY

Class: Graphic Design
and Computer Graphics
Level: Second Year
Faculty: Maurizio Osti and Danilo Danisi
Duration of Project: Two Semesters

PROJECT BRIEF

Students are charged with developing a new identity system for the academy to reflect changes in the organizational structure and enhanced communication courses initiated in 2004, according to the reforms proposed by the Italian Ministry of Education. Three departments have been launched; new courses are now offered not only in the fine arts but also in graphic design, product design, scenography, restoration, communication arts, and so on. The logo has to maintain the institutional icon: the academy's *Fama*, a very important masterpiece by Marcantonio Franceschini; so the whole project must respect this particular element. Three groups of students are to design the institutional part of the entire communication system: logo, stationery, signage systems, posters, and merchandising.

PROJECT OUTCOME

The projects will be examined by a jury composed of the Academy's president, director, and academic board. The best project will become the official identity system for the institute and will be used for both internal communications and external operations.

↑ Logo designs and applications

Students: Second-year graphic design class

The class redesigned the classic logo, playing with different styles.

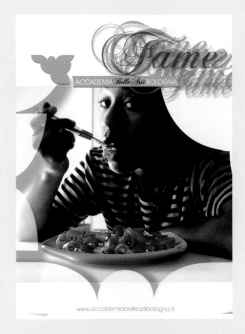

↑ Student: Diana Blankson

Photograph: Francesca Coppola

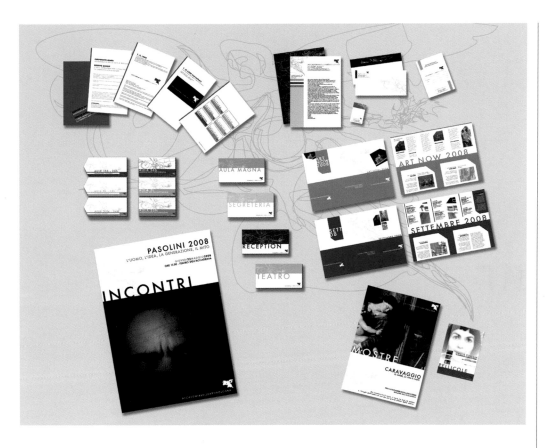

↑ Students: Andrea Vernucci, Serena Muratori, Nadia Pantaleoni, and Laura Gruppuso

← Students: Elena La Placa, Barbara Pavone, Lorena D'alfonso, and Francesca Coppola

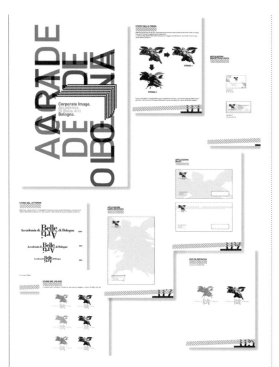

↑ Student: Daniele Asteggiante
Photograph: Nicola Medri

↑ Student: Daniele Asteggiante

← Student: Elena La Placa
Photograph: Diana Blankson

Boston and Suzhou: A Cultural Concept Book Study

Boston University, School of Visual Arts/ Suzhou Art and Design Technology Institute

BOSTON, MASSACHUSETTS, USA/SUZHOU, SOOCHOW, CHINA

PROJECT BRIEF

Study the materials I've brought from Boston, including postcards of Boston landmarks, stamps, newspapers, assorted Red Sox paraphernalia, and Boston Marathon bib numbers and medals. Scan and photocopy the Boston material and combine it with your own photographic images and illustrations from Suzhou, including hand drawings, painting, and digital photography. Use the text from Henry Wadsworth Longfellow's "Paul Revere's Ride" and Ralph Waldo Emerson's "Boston," to explore alternate methods of visualizing narration: continuous text, typographic expression, diagrams, timelines, map construction, and text/image combinations. You may use either English text or Chinese calligraphy or a combination of the two. Focus on the cinematic aspects of multipage design, unity, pacing, contrast, and rhythm. The cultural concept book should be small and intimate in nature and should not exceed 8 × 10 inches (20.5 × 25.5 cm). The book should be a minimum of eight pages in length, including the front and back covers.

PROJECT GOAL

The objective of the workshop is to compare and contrast the Western and Eastern cities of Boston and Suzhou by taking a closer look at these two cities' personalities. Although Suzhou, located thirty two miles northwest of Shanghai, is a large modern city, one can find a network of sixteenth-century canals, bridges, and classical gardens. Students are challenged to think about how living in or visiting a city influences the way we think and see. Create short, multipage books integrating images from both Boston and Suzhou that would visually communicate the similarities and differences in the visual culture of the two cities. Think about how you'll visually

Class: A Cultural Concept Book Workshop
Level: Junior and Senior
Faculty: Richard B. Doubleday
Duration of Project: One Week

convey the mood and temperament of the subject matter and your experiences in Suzhou and, conversely, your impressions of Boston.

PROJECT OUTCOME

The final designs comprised a variety of cultural concept books, depicting famous Chinese water townships, expressive typography, postcard images, statues, Boston architecture, and Chinese "stamp" motifs. The students spent the first two days working through preliminary ideas and drafting rough sketches. The second half of the week was spent creating the books and completing the project. The results combined Eastern and Western imagery with English text and Chinese calligraphy to form a unique and unusual juxtaposition of design elements. The two class critiques enabled the students to get instantaneous feedback, critique their classmates' design solutions, and articulate the ideas behind their own projects.

↑ Student: Qi Huang

↑ Student: Zhubian Yang Jie

↑ Student: Xuleyi

I merged contemporary Boston and classical Chinese architecture.

↑ Student: Zhang Meile

The stamp motifs are ancient Chinese folk designs that have been in use for many centuries. The symbols comprise *hua yang* patterns and represent long life, riches, etc. I cut freehand forms from paper with scissors and overlaid the stamp motifs for each page within the book.

↑ Student: Qian Dan Dan

I created a colorful and vibrant collage effect, documenting each day of the week.

↑ Student: Mengjing Cao

Water, Politics, and Hope

Brigham Young University (BYU)

PROVO, UTAH, USA

12

Class: Special Problems in Graphic Design
Level: Senior
Faculty: Linda Sullivan
Duration of Project: One Semester

PROJECT BRIEF

The class assignment was to choose a national or international social issue that could be universally shared and individually articulated.

PROJECT GOAL

Water carries a host of connotations. Nations hoard the riches of their rivers and reservoirs. Irrigation canals branch across arid fields like veins of economic lifeblood for millions of farmers. The Nile nourishes crops with fertile soil deposits. In 1970, the Egyptian government dammed the river to secure more land for its burgeoning population. The twist of a valve brings limitless gallons of water pouring through hoses, showers, and sinks. A few months of drought turn suburban lawns a desiccated yellow. In Africa, a child dies after only a few days without water. An avalanche in the Rocky Mountains buries a hiker in ice. A tsunami inundates Thailand with water, drowning thousands. In Hong Kong, monsoons flood the streets with mud. An oil spill in the Pacific poisons fish and dolphins. Water rights create grudges, lawsuits, and wars.

Beyond its associations with politics, fear, and death, water can also symbolize home and life. Inside their mother's womb, babies swim and grow immersed in water. Water energizes, relieves, cleanses, and feeds. During the summer, children run through sprinklers or flock to water parks. Tourists travel from around the world to gawk at Niagara Falls. A Christian is reborn through the waters of baptism, and a grieving family in India sprinkles cremated ashes on the waters of the Ganges. The comfort, awe, and sanctity of water runs alongside its tense politics and cutthroat economics. Its changing significance and meanings continually circulate beneath society, like the groundwater below the earth.

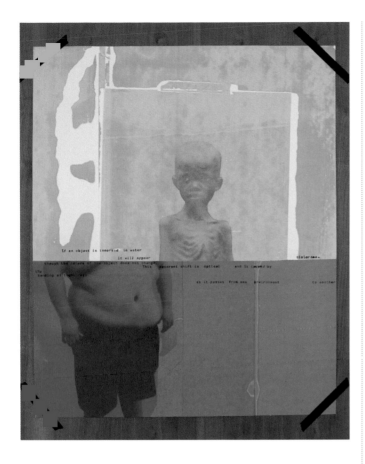

← Refraction

Student: Jon Troutman

Our view of the world is often a divided one. Rich. Poor. Educated. Uneducated. Familiar. Foreign. Good. Bad. Black. White. Us. Them. We don't see the human race as a singular unit with inherent, internal connections. Rather, we focus on external signifiers and draw distorted conclusions and judgments— whether subconscious or deliberate. Our skewed view of each other is contrary to God's holistic view of us. With a more holistic perspective, we might see humanity as an equal organism that lives, breathes, and stretches throughout a host of unequal environments.

← Come Again Another Day

Student: Jeremy Bowen

It is intriguing that in our culture where there is abundant access to clean water, associations with rain are largely negative. Rain is inconvenient and depressing— in other words, "bad weather." Movies, for example, constantly use rain to communicate sadness, loneliness, fear, and even death. In this piece, I'm bringing attention to its beautiful, positive, and life-giving qualities.

← Advertising for Water, Politics and Hope

Students: Keenan Cummings and Jon Troutman
To promote the exhibit "Water, Politics and Hope"

→ Don't Drink the Water

Student: Angie Panian

The Clean Water Act is the primary piece of legislation controlling water pollution in this country. What many people don't know is that the Clean Water Act is in trouble; recent changes passed by the Supreme Court under the Bush administration have weakened this law. They have changed the definition of the waters protected under the act, putting a large number of America's rivers, streams, and lakes at risk for the first time since the law was passed in 1977. But this doesn't have to continue. The Clean Water Restoration Act of 2007 has been introduced and is now in the first step of the legislative process.

← From Water to Oil and Back

Student: Keenan Cummings

Water and oil have always been sources for life, struggle, hope, contention, and energy. Both hold strong cultural, social, and political symbolism. "From Water to Oil and Back" is a personal look at these symbols and how they have developed over time. For two chemicals that are so fundamentally opposite, they share a very similar place in our lives.

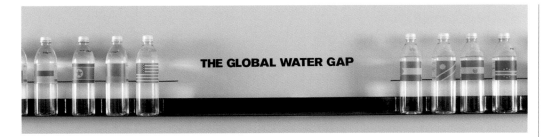

↑ The Global Water Gap

Student: Nick Mendoza

The Koran says, "By means of water we give life to everything." This simple teaching captures a deeper wisdom. People need water as surely as they need oxygen: without it, life could not exist. But water also gives life in a far broader sense. People need clean water and sanitation to sustain their health and maintain their dignity. But beyond the household, water also sustains ecological systems and provides an input into the production systems that maintain livelihoods. Ultimately, human development is about the realization of potential. It is about what people can do and what they can become—their capabilities—and about the freedom they have to exercise real choices in their lives. When people are denied access to clean water at home or when they lack access to water as a productive resource, their choices and freedoms are constrained by ill health, poverty, and vulnerability. Water gives life to everything, including human development and human freedom.

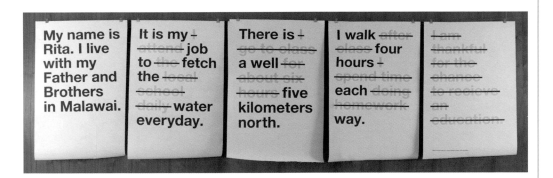

↑ Rita

Student: Tyler Smart

No child should have to make the choice between having clean water to drink and getting an education. Unfortunately, many children in Africa face this decision daily. Their education suffers both from the time they are forced to spend acquiring water and from the poor facilities in schools due to a lack of water. We can help put an end to these terrible circumstances.

→ The Tributary

Student: Arlo Vance

When discussing consumption, the first thing that comes to mind is not how much water I actually use; it usually has something to do with whether or not I'm recycling the disposable cup from the Venti Soy Latté I bought at Starbucks. Living in a society where overconsumption is the norm, it is no wonder that we are concerned about things for which the rest of the world has little care. So many people in the world do not have the daily requirements of water for living, let alone conveniences.

↓ Water Is Blood

Student: Zack Bartlett

Earth is the body; water is the blood. The veins flow through the body as rivers and creeks, leading to the ocean. Poisoning the bloodstream will kill the body. Our waste, which ends up in city runoff, eventually reaches the ocean.

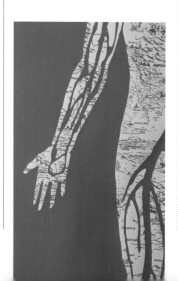

↑ Umbrellas

Student: Jenny Willardson

I think it is significant that in the United States we have something designed to shield us from the rain. But in many underdeveloped countries life depends on the rainwater received. I thought the different orientations of the umbrella were an appropriate symbol of how we avoid the rain and how others collect it.

→ **Africa Is Evaporating**

Student: Kevin Cantrell

Drought has played a major role in the history of Africa; it has erased lakes and rivers, thus greatly impacting societies and families. "Africa Is Evaporating" addresses the effects of drought in Africa at an individual level: Due to the lack of clean drinking water, people, like lakes and rivers, are dissipating. Although we cannot control the weather, we can ensure that Africa has clean drinking water.

Town of Split Workshop

Arts Academy of Split, Department of Visual Communications

SPLIT, CROATIA

Class: Graphic Design
Level: Fifth Semester
Faculty: Ljubica Marcetic Marinovic
Duration of Project: One Semester

PROJECT BRIEF

The theme of the workshop is the town of Split. Each student selects one area somehow related to Split and its particulars (culture, geography, history, sociology). After having carried out research, on the basis of analysis, the student independently conceives innovations that contribute to the quality of urban living. The concepts should be simple and cost effective to implement.

PROJECT GOAL

The workshop's objective is to stimulate students to actively observe the surroundings in which they study as a collection of living processes and changes. During the workshop, the student discovers and recognizes parts of structural, organizational, sociological, and economic relations, independently identifies problems, stagnations, or advantages, and tries to give a creative answer to them for the well-being of the entire community.

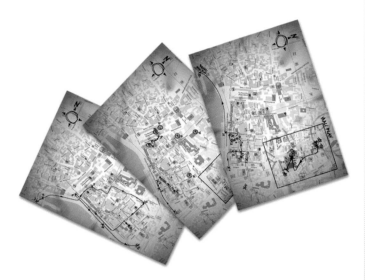

← Split's Way

Student: Marko Svraka

This visual guide is like having a friend in Split who has written instructions on how to spend time in the town and which places you have to visit, regardless of who you are or what your interests. The contents of this guide, visual and otherwise, were created using an "old time" theme and in the spirit of the local dialect, which is why the "way" becomes more than just a stroll through the streets of town, it becomes entertaining, subjective, and personal.

← Siti se Siti
(*Remember, Remember*)

Student: Matea Pavkovic

Siti se Siti is a game intended for preschool children and lower elementary school students. It is based on the principle of memory games, and its objective is to nurture local dialect and its comparison with Croatian literary language. On one side, the cards have initial letters of the concepts illustrated on the back side. The words in Split's dialect are hidden behind words written in big capital letters, while the words from literary language are hidden behind small letters. The game is endless, as a child can play for as long as she likes by turning the cards over and playing the opposite way. The game was featured on a national educational program.

↑ Imperator

Student: Tomislav Cubelic

The game Imperator was created as a consequence of the current state of poor zoning and illegal construction in Split, even in the old part of town, Diocletian Palace. The objective of the game is to feel the ease with which something of historical and cultural importance can be purchased and sold for material gain. The game uses three currencies—money, luck, and knowledge of the town. The game is a copy of everyday life in Split. The work has been published in *Novum* magazine and was featured on a national television program.

← Diocletian's Recipes
Student: Klementina Tadin

This cultural and culinary picture of Dalmatia, rooted in mythical antics, today shapes the basis of everyday living. By collecting recipes from Split's housewives and chefs, I recalled the pictures of full, satisfied smiles from lunches with family and friends. The recipes are printed on postcards and distributed free of charge at all spots where homemade food can be purchased. The project's objective is for people to remember their heritage and start eating healthily for less money.

→ Impulse
Student: Ante Klai

Impulse is an installation that unites sociology, architecture, electrical engineering, and design. The project is conceptualized as a prototype for lighting narrow streets in the city center. By emphasizing specific Mediterranean urbanism and interaction, this type of lighting would provide Split with a special visual code. On entering an alley, passers-by activate a hidden sensor by which the lights begin to switch on slowly, illuminating their way. After passing, the lights are programmed to slowly switch off. This gives an impression of an impulse by which we revive the town of Split on a daily basis, by flowing through its veins/streets.

← Split's Way

Student: Nikola Radovani

Split's Way draws attention to interesting details that average people don't notice while walking the streets. Due to increasing congestion, jams, and hastiness, we don't notice those little interesting things that could spice up our routine. This project intends to bring attention to details; to motivate walkers to think about problems they encounter on their way; and to stimulate them to discover some new, interesting things.

→ Soap and Water calendar

Student: Igor Carli

Contrary to the usual practice of putting the most beautiful images on calendars, this calendar depicts the problems in the town center. It features photographs of garbage on city streets, inappropriately installed air-conditioners, stone benches that are too cold for people to sit on, endless lines of TV antennas, illegally parked cars, etc. The objective is to divert the attention of citizens and municipal institutions from photographs carefully processed in Photoshop and make them start paying attention to the real picture of the city.

My First Political Poster Design: Chile, the Other September 11th

Maryse Eloy School of Art/ University of Art and Design Helsinki

PARIS, FRANCE/HELSINKI, FINLAND

14

Class: Visual Communication: Semiology
Level: Third Year
Faculty: François Caspar
Duration of Project: Four Weeks

Class: International Workshop
Level: Fifth Year
Faculty: François Caspar
Duration of Project: One Week

PROJECT BRIEF

Students should research and collect images that represent and memorialize the events of September 11, 2001, from the point of view both of Chile and New York City. The collected images can be of small size on a sketchbook. The goal is to compare how the media in both countries portrayed the event, how the audiences reacted, how it impacted the different societies, and how it is commemorated or forgotten today. Students will bring the result of their inquiries (found images and texts) and their sketches (black and white, 4 × 6 inches [10 × 15 cm]) to class for open discussion. The posters will show the outcome of this comparison.

PROJECT GOAL

Following the New York event, like many people, I had to express my empathy, but I was too shocked to do so right after. I did it one year later, for its first commemoration: As a designer, I made a poster. But as a person forty years of age, I thought of Chile on September 11, 1973, when president Salvador Allende was overthrown by the military and democracy, as we knew it, died. I was too young at the time to remember it. Today, I am interested to see how younger people who were not born then respond to and visually depict this part of history and what links they may find to that time. I want to know what our memory gets or forgets. What do we commemorate or lose? To create a sharp and smart image, the students have

to collect archival images, to see the works of preceding graphic designers. The challenge is not to create a new image commemorating either the Chilean event or the American one, but, rather, an image that compares them. This should help the students be more aware of their role as designers in our societies.

Poster designs, students from Paris

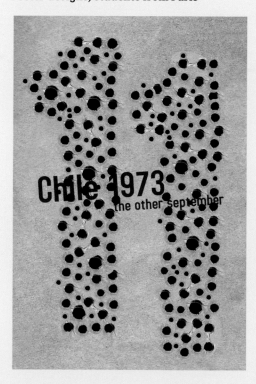

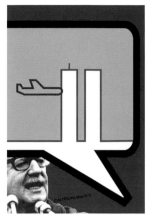

↑ Student: Violette De Fleurian

↑ Student: Tina Bourade

↑ Student: Timothée Silie

↑ Student: Mirabelle Pezier

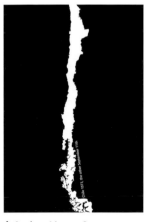

↑ Student: Morgan Serre

↑ Student: Noélie Briey

← Student: Madison Renegez

↑ Student: Fanny Chansard

↑ Student: Claire Roche

Poster designs, students from Helsinki

↑ Student: Aki Scharin

↑ Student: Eva Neesemann

↑ Student: Heidi Gabrielsson

↑ Student: Johannes Naan

↑ Student: Juha Juvonen

↑ Student: Michael Muyanja

↑ Student: Pablo Ferreiro

↑ Student: Sima Utku

↑ Student: Anton Yarkin

↑ Student: Gibran Julian

↑ Student: Hannele Torro

↑ Student: Veronika Schmidt

To Die For

Fabrica, the Benetton Group Research Center

TREVISO, ITALY

15

Contributors: Namyoung Ann, Michael Ciancio, Scott Heinrich, Priyadarshini Khatri, Edward Tad Kimball, Piero Martinello, Daniel Streat, Lars Wannop, and Parick Waterhouse

Project Director: Omar Vulpinari, Head of Visual Communication
Duration of Project: Six Weeks

PROJECT BRIEF

In Spring 2007, *The Walrus* asked Fabrica to comment on visually and raise awareness of the Darfur humanitarian crisis. This Canadian magazine is intellectually rigorous, politically engaged, and committed to the use of excellent imagery.

The preliminary brief from the magazine's creative director, Antonio De Luca, and picture editor, Bree Seeley, was very stimulating and challenging. It required us to focus the commentary on those decadent Western world distractions that keep the developed countries from acting concretely against the crisis. The brief stated:

"There is a fundamental lack of urgency to protect the most vulnerable on our planet. The size of the crisis in Darfur mocks our civility. We want to make our readership painfully aware of the number of innocents killed in this crisis, the veritable malice of the Sudanese central government showing through the unwillingness to protect its people, highlight the 'sub-plots' of mass rape, sickness and hunger which pour out of the displaced/refugee population situation, and also illuminate the sources backing the Janjaweed.

We wish to point generally (or specifically) to aspects of our western culture that distract us from addressing the genocide (celebrity media, housing boom, designer objects . . .).

Thereby ask yourselves; 'what on earth does it take' to see the rich West accept part responsibility for the prolonging of immense suffering. To address our value system and lay it bare. Whether this is done through the design of symbols, plain text, through juxtapositions of imagery, history or whatever, we are open to your inventions."

PROJECT GOAL

The Walrus creative team asked Fabrica to design a powerful poster addressing the crisis in Darfur that readers could tear out of the publication. The message of the poster should make readers aware of the urgency of the Darfur crisis and let them know they can do something to help the suffering.

PROJECT OUTCOME

A group of Fabricans from the areas of visual communication, photography, and product design were engaged for six weeks, working in teams and individually. Critiques and research-sharing meetings were frequent and packed with intense debate around the cultural, political, and geographic specifics of the Darfur crisis, but primarily concentrated on determining what could be the most emotionally impacting messages for *The Walrus* readership. The final result was a multiauthor, eight-page visual essay published in the September 2008 issue.

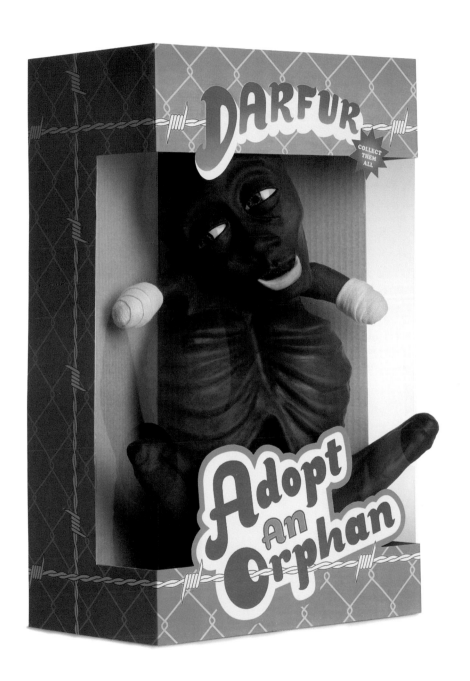

↑ Student: Scott Heinrich

Photograph: Piero Martinello

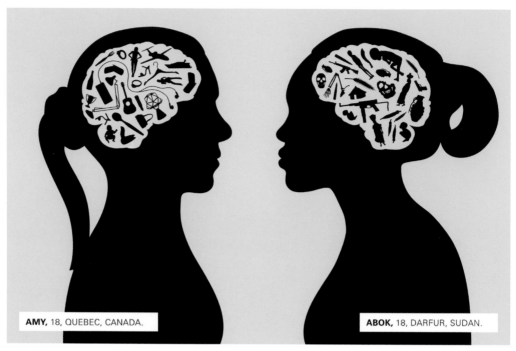

↑ Student: Daniel Steat

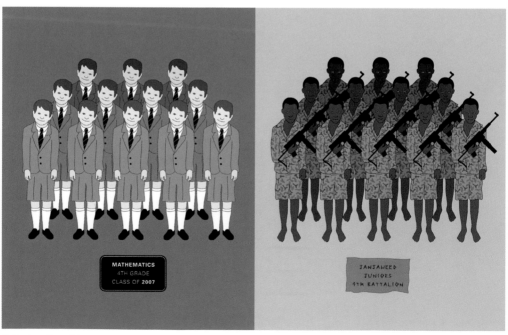

↑ Student: Daniel Sreat

↑ Student: Michael Ciancio. Photograph: Piero Martinello

↑ Student: Priyadarshini Khatri. Photograph: Piero Martinello

↑ Student: Namyoung Ann

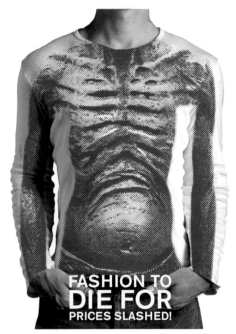

↑ Student: Michael Ciancio. Photograph: Piero Martinello

South African Stories

Red and Yellow School of Logic and Magic/ Stellenbosch University

CAPE TOWN, SOUTH AFRICA/MATIELAND, SOUTH AFRICA

16

Class: Graphic Design
Level: Second Year
Faculty: Gabby Raaf

PROJECT BRIEF

"South African Stories" was the theme of Orange Juice Design's experimental graphics magazine *i-Jusi* (issue 24) in late 2007. Contributors were asked to write a five hundred-word short story to accompany their design for the cover. The cover needed to reflect a real book, such as one would encounter in any commercial bookstore. The story had to depict a typical South African encounter, experience, or fantasy.

PROJECT GOAL

- Encourage designers to try their hand at creative writing.
- Experience and report on a South African–inspired personal story.
- Design a book cover with commercial appeal.

iGolide

Student: Sifiso Taleni

Who said that a dentist could be only someone with dental qualifications? Here in Mzansi (South Africa), in the black townships and skwatta , we have unqualified dentists who perform dental operations just like qualified dentists!

In the township of KwaMakhuta where I live, I met an *umjita* (fellow), Simphiwe Khoza, who calls himself the Crown Dentist of the neighborhood and probably even the whole of KwaMakhuta township, which is close to Amanzimtoti.

His target market is teenagers who want gold and silver crowns, but don't have the money to go to a qualified dentist. Simphiwe performs his operations with a pair of scissors and pliers, cans of Coke and cans of Castle Lager out of his two-room home.

The inside of the Coca-Cola can acts as the silver crown and the inside of the Castle can acts as the gold crown. He cuts the cans along the sides and throws away the top and bottom because they are hard and not flat, which makes them unusable. He then flattens the sides of the cans with a steel-and-wooden roller so that it becomes 100 percent straight. When the cans are flattened they are cut into $\frac{1}{8} \times \frac{1}{8}$ inch (3 × 3 mm) pieces with a pair of scissors and packed away for the clients, safely under the bed or inside the wardrobe.

During the operation, you have to open your mouth wide while you sit on an uncomfortable wooden stool that has pieces of cushion on it. He measures your tooth by placing the $\frac{1}{8} \times \frac{1}{8}$ inch (3 x 3 mm) piece of can on your tooth and he keeps clipping the piece with the scissors until he finds the size to fit. When he has found the right size, he makes folds with the pliers and clips the side onto your tooth with the pliers.

When you have to eat you unclip the crown and take it out of your mouth, so that you don't have to damage your crown—or even worse—swallow your crown with the food.

The crowns are cleaned with brass metal cleaner to keep them shiny, but the more you use it, the more it will permanently lose its color. The cost of the operation is R70, while a qualified dentist with the "real" crown will charge you between R1000 and R2000. In Mzansi, some people find a way to make almost anything that is considered popular and expensive accessible to those with a low income!

Carmageddon and Bergie-Flavored Roadkill

Student: Adri Goosen

And so I ran him over, unintentionally of course. And back to front—subconsciously somehow choosing to maim while in reverse. Can I do nothing right? But be it backward chance or forward rage, the simple fact remains that I drove over a living, breathing, probably hallucinating, nonetheless human being. Flesh and blood vs. steel.

I've heard rumors about the flexibility of a drunken body, but drunk or not, the sound is the same. You hear it in the movies when hero-steered cars drive over entranced zombies, making roadkill of their putrid flesh. It's like a dove hitting the windscreen, only a hundred times worse. The dull thud of flesh going limp, of muscles straining, tearing, blood vessels popping . . . An instant stretches out to hold a thousand helpless heartbeats and two worlds collide slowly, almost soundlessly until a living corpse limply embraces its fate and from beyond the silence comes that awful sound. Phantom raises stricken face and goes down . . . Murderer.

The moment is blood-curdling, life-altering. And you know you're screwed. One white female with a politically incorrect heritage maims one politically correct colored male—a mere zombie shuffling along aimlessly, entranced by imaginary fiends, brain-matter putrid from too many benzene-filled nights. Scum of society, social castaway, drunkard. But blood flows, you know, it flows to stain the hands of those that spill it. Regardless of how diluted that blood may be, it is blood. Or so our constitution argues. But who really gives a shit about the blood of a bergie. South African annoyance, one less to haunt our streets, screeching damnation upon law-abiding, hardworking citizens. But none of that matters. All that matters is that I am the white perpetrator, he is the black victim and . . . Fuck! A benzene-soaked bergie, natural hazard drifting into sight as if on the sea breeze, just ruined my life . . . I just killed a bergie—the realization enshrouds me . . . I just killed a human being . . . Oh shit.

Why did he have to be black? Why could he not be white? Unintentional manslaughter of white men is okay. No one follows up on those, heck, no one even follows up the intentional ones. Fuck fuck fuck, fuck, fuck. . . . Something moves as if from a great distance and I turn to look into blood-shot, empty eyes. Face against the glass, the zombie grimaces, displaying rotten teeth, hungry tongue. Dead man walking, I scream. But zombie simply steps away and smiles a senseless smile, wrinkling up his leathery face, front teeth now harmlessly missing. And then he wanders off, alive. I try to stop him, but he is chasing some invisible villain, complaining eloquently about some unjust treatment, a blue banana and Saartjie's seven-headed dog. I drive off, rattled, relieved, confused that metal did not triumph over drug-sodden muscle.

Much later, my proudly politically incorrect brother phones to pounce upon my confusion and applaud my patriotism, "Congratulations, Mrs. ANC," he smugly growls, "you're finally one of us. You nearly killed yourself a kaffir."

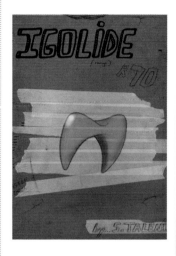

↑ Student: Sifiso Taleni

↑ Student: Adri Goosen

The Formal Language of a Display Typeface

Iceland Academy of the Arts

REYKJAVIK, ICELAND

17

Class: Forms and Ideas 1
Level: Third (Final) Year
Faculty: Goddur
Duration of Project: Eight Weeks

PROJECT BRIEF

Design a new display typeface based on an existing typeface. Expand the formal language of this new typeface into a visual system that encompasses the underlying ideas and objectives. Create a brand using the microcosm of forms and ideas already designed.

PROJECT GOAL

How a graphic designer becomes a god: Over the course of some years, Goddur's class has been experimenting with an exercise in identity creation based on form by making a display typeface the starting point for holistic graphic design. The idea is to research an existing typeface and its context (visually, theoretically, socially, and historically) and its author and the author's background, then create a contemporary display typeface based on the outcome of the research. The new typeface becomes the basis for identity creation for an entity such as a company, ideology, or anything it can fully communicate in a contemporary manner. This is then explored further in branding exercises, but without the restraints of commercial concerns. So the experiment becomes an exercise where function follows form. The designer becomes god, and creation is his sole objective. The designer is then free to design a microcosm to suit his ideas.

PROJECT OUTCOME

Based on their research, the students have made typefaces that have evolved into their own visual vocabularies and translated the formal language of the typeface into comprehensive and contemporary identity projects. We see a strong current of type design based on an underlying system—the grid. There are also many designs based on modular systems. This is an interesting development because our visual heritage is based mostly on two elements: the written word (literature and handwritten, illuminated scripts) and embroidery, knitting, and needlework. These are, of course, closely related to the grid. Iceland is young and therefore it is critical at this point to explore and expand our visual identity as a whole—but do so based on our legacy.

→ **Everything Typeface**
Student: Helgi Pall Einarsson

This is a modular typeface designed to be assembled at random by a computer.

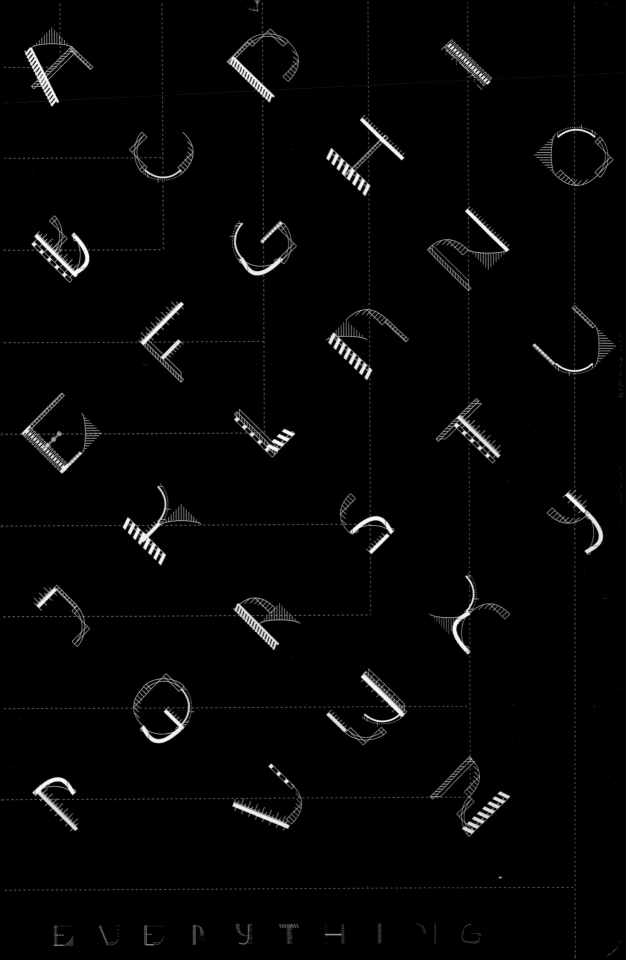

EVERYTHING

→ SEXKANT Typeface

Student: Daniel Claus Reuter

The vision of the SEXKANT typeface is to create a better everyday life for many people. We make this possible by offering a wide range of well-designed, functional letters at prices so low that as many people as possible will be able to afford them.

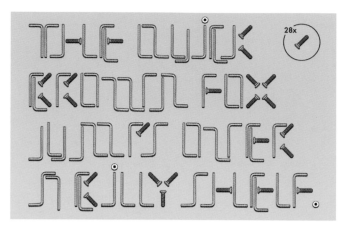

→ Morthens Typeface

Student: Jonas Valtysson

I decided to use a script typeface called Vitrina by Pablo Medina. I chose it because I liked the method Pablo used to create it. He takes pictures of his urban surroundings and bases his design on them.

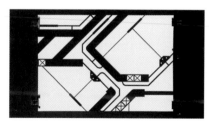

→ Grindavík Typeface

Student: Sveinn Davidsson

Grindavík is a monospaced typeface that comes in three weights. It was inspired by Wim Crouwel's type design, Futhark runes, and older comae forms.

QUICK, JAB MY FADING PINK ZIT, EVIL SEX WHORE!

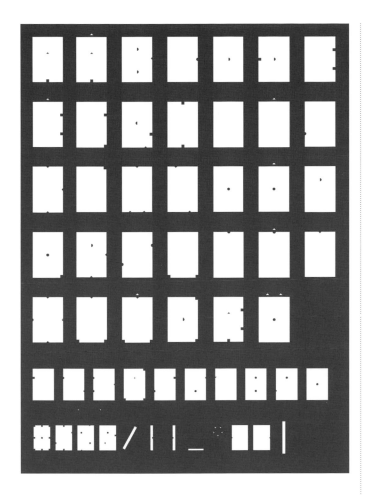

↑ Basic Typeface

Student: Ragnar Freyr Palsson

This is an attempt to make the simplest typeface using only the basic forms. The result is minimal yet very loud. Funnily enough, this typeface is based on Franklin Gothic.

↑ Dingleballs Typeface

Student: Birna Geirfinnsdottir

I created this font after researching Paul Renner's Futura.

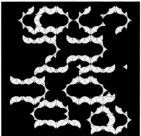

↑ Snidagrind and Kogra Typefaces

Student: Siggi Oddsson

Snidagrind is inspired by Stephan Muller's Gateway. It mimics the modular grid of the typeface, while being much more complex and organic. It comes in two types, A and B, and within each type is a version for both small and large sizes. Kogra was inspired by fractals and is intended for use in large sizes.

↑ Veekend, Father, and Abkur Typefaces

Student: Geir Helgi Birgisson

Visualizing Various Information Types across Multiple Channels

Illinois Institute of Technology, Institute of Design

CHICAGO, ILLINOIS, USA

Class: Communication Design Workshop
Level: Masters
Faculty: Tomoko Ichikawa
Duration of Project: Seven to Fifteen Weeks

PROJECT BRIEF

Communication often occurs in multiple formats. The purpose of this project is to have students convey complex information in several distinct formats. In this class, students are required to be researchers, authors, editors, and designers. A good amount of class time is spent on content development where the students explore the essence of the story to determine its inherent structure. From there, they represent this structure in visual form, allowing the viewer to engage with the content in a way that is accessible at first glance and easy to comprehend. Students are responsible for choosing a topic within the domain of physical health and well-being, researching and developing content, and designing the final pieces. Along the way, they are asked to examine the differences between the formats and to work with the characteristics of each. Such characteristics deal with the sequential/holistic, viewer-controlled/presenter-controlled, permanent/ephemeral nature of each. Students are challenged to consider design issues such as narration and sequence, visual hierarchy, progressive disclosure, cognitive preparation through advanced organizers, matching of content structure to visual structure, units of viewing, and information density.

PROJECT GOAL

Projects will be designed in three different formats: booklet, poster, and a slidelike presentation. The topic for the initial project will address physical health and well-being; subsequent topics

can be areas where the student already has ample knowledge. We will also conduct an audit of existing visualizations to analyze the project's success (or lack thereof), and examine design principles used and possible alternate solutions.

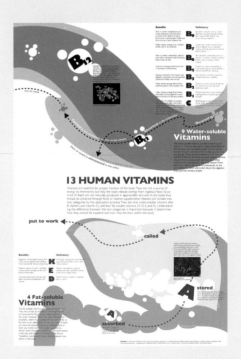

↑ Human Vitamins

Student: Kyungsun Kim

The challenge, when trying to describe the world of vitamins, is solved by dividing the thirteen vitamins into two basic groups: water soluble and fat soluble. This became the basic structure for my poster and booklet. The poster uses two very dynamic, abstract images of water and liver/intestines to represent the absorption process of the two groups. The poster also outlines the benefits and deficiencies of each vitamin.

↓ Scoliosis

Student: Phillip LaFargue II

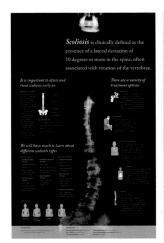

Benefiting from a dramatic image that visually describes scoliosis, viewers are shown how to detect the condition early, understanding of the various types of scoliosis, and major treatment options. Clear and simple structuring of the content, effective use of typographical hierarchy, and informative graphics in each of the sections result in an easy-to-view poster.

↑ Biotechnology versus Organic Food Production

Student: Lucas Daniel

By demonstrating comparative information of two opposing types of food production and distribution, this poster attempts to educate on various levels. In what is essentially an annotated and illustrated matrix, the viewer sees comparisons at each step (indicated in the middle column in gray) from production to market. The introductory paragraphs on top under the "Biotechnology" and "Organic" headings, along with the text between the two faces, synthesize the big story that sets up the remaining content in the poster. A comparative timeline appears at the bottom to indicate major milestones of each production method.

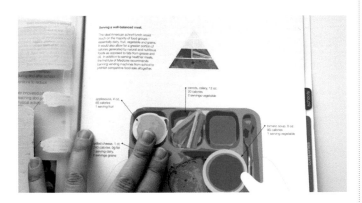

↑ Childhood Obesity

Student: Jessica Gatto

My poster compares daily activities of families in the U.S. with obese parents and those with nonobese parents in the U.S. Activities include eating together, being active as a family, and television viewing. Contrasting the body mass index of the two groups from toddler age to young adulthood is also revealing. Comparisons are done in a nonjudgmental fashion, allowing viewers to arrive at conclusions on their own. My booklet provides a more sequential narrative. It outlines societal factors that contribute to obesity—a steeper increase in carbohydrate consumption versus protein consumption, a more rapid rise in the price index of produce versus soft drinks and sweets, and a decrease in walking and biking—and offers solution areas, calling on parents, schools, and the media.

X Box

Istanbul Bilgi University, Department of Visual Communication Design

ISTANBUL, TURKEY

Class: Publication Design
Level: Second Year
Faculty: Esen Karol
Duration of Project: One Semester

PROJECT BRIEF

X Box is a monthly periodical. Its "cover" is its box and it contains a magazine, a book, a catalogue, and at least one ephemeral item (e.g., a sticker, a postcard). "X" depends on the topic, which is chosen by the student: Music Box, History Box, Porn Box, and Soccer Box alike. The students are expected to design the complete box by making the necessary editorial decisions. All the publications and ephemera coming out of the box have to be related to the chosen topic and to each other. The project results in a mock-up, which includes all of the elements and is to be documented photographically. The issue of the so-called neutrality of the designer is to be questioned. Development of a personal perspective is important. For the magazine, the student has to design a short article (minimum two pages), a long article (minimum six pages), an interview (minimum two pages), news pages (minimum two pages), contents page (minimum one page), and the cover. The student is expected to work in the given order starting with short article pages and finishing with the cover. The editorial conventions of magazine production are to be questioned. For the book, the student has to design at least four sample pages, divider pages if necessary, half title, title, contents, colophon, and the cover. For the catalogue, the student should design at least four sample pages besides the divider, title and content pages, and the cover. The conventions of categorization are to be questioned. The book and the catalogue can be a

redesign of an existing book; however, the magazine is expected to be a new product; the sort of publication the student wishes existed.

PROJECT GOAL

By working on three kinds of publications in one semester the students are introduced to the primary issues in designing for print. A magazine, a catalogue, and a book have very different qualities although they all happen to consist of many pages. They are produced with different intentions, are read differently, and they take on different functions after their initial consumption. By making all the editorial decisions, the students become aware of the complexities of the structure of these media. Also by having to relate each publication to the others, students learn how to approach a whole, which consists of individual parts. Students are primarily engaged in moving images, so they are encouraged to design as if they are editing a film.

→ Post Box Magazine
Student: Serkan Arslan

Post Box Magazine is about design culture, and every month it will be sent to people's post boxes. While working on the layout, I tried to use the photographs as large as I could. I want the readers to have an idea about the content as soon as they are confronted with a page. I've used white background and thin black lines and tried to keep the layout simple. I also used stock vector postal symbols on the corners of pages, which I think go well with concept of magazine.

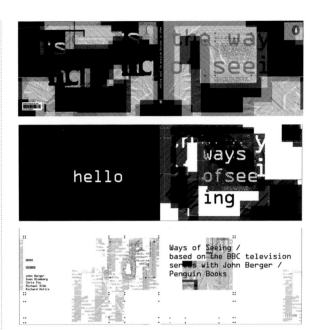

↑ **Ways of Seeing**

Student: Efe Mert Kaya

My project is a redesign of John Berger's *Ways of Seeing*. It consists of a series of written and visual essays that raises questions about hidden ideologies in visual images. With the help of a hex editor, I've created random glitches in the visual material of the book, including the publisher's logo. This approach can be considered another way of seeing.

← **Annual Catalog of Actar**

Student: Kaan Ficici

This annual catalog of books published by Actar displays a lot of information in a limited space. Readers can navigate according to their personal interests. At the same time, books from different sections can be compared to one another. Since each book has an individual space, they are differentiated, and the information on a specific book can be torn from the catalog.

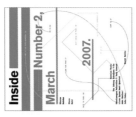

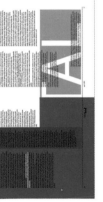

← ImprovBox

Student: Okay Karadayilar

ImprovBox magazine is about improvised music, featuring artists and offering a variety of essays and reviews. It is a part of *ImprovBox*, a quarterly offering containing the magazine, a catalogue of related miscellanea, a book, and some stickers. Though the usual bits and pieces of a regular magazine are present, the juxtaposition of the elements mimics the experience of listening to improvised music.

← HalluBox

Student: Ceren Atalay

HalluBox is a magazine on the art of illustration. I think that there are a lot of life objects situated somewhere between reality and abstraction. I used very few illustrations and instead I played with the image of typography. I made use of strong color contrasts and deformed words to imply this merging of reality and abstraction. That is why the subject of the magazine became the lost object of reality, but in the eye of the beholder it has a hallucinating effect, as the name implies.

← Peripteral

Student: Refik Anadol

Peripteral is a monthly magazine containing a variety of articles on architecture, architectural photography, design, and the elements of each. Typefaces are chosen according to the articles. Monochrome color is preferred for all typographic and graphic elements and applied in different ways depending on articles. I've experimented with photography throughout the magazine, searching for different aesthetic qualities in the images.

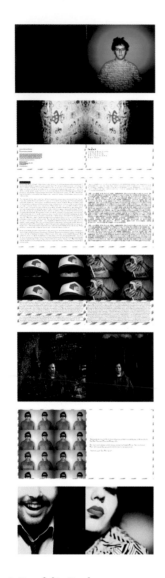

↑ **Portfolio Book**

Student: Maurizio Braggiotti

Portfolio Book is about my personal work. The book includes a series of portraits that were taken with a medium-format camera. For this reason, the book has the shape of a square. Since it is a personal project, I've preferred to use my own handwriting instead of an existing typeface.

↑ **CameoBox**

Student: Ceyhun Saracoglu

CameoBox, a monthly film culture magazine, refers to a cameo appearance. Since films try to illustrate reality on the screen, I used illustrations instead of photography. By doing so, I think I've managed to illustrate the reality of the film on the printed page and to capture the soul of the content.

↑ **Street Box**

Student: Alican Akturk

Street Box is a street art and graffiti magazine for practitioners. I tried to keep the design as tidy as possible by using a three-column grid system. The works of the artists are presented as bleeding images. White space is avoided.

← The Process

Student: Akin Gulseven

Additional Credit: Text by Mark Nelson,
Carolyn G. Quertin, Hasso Krull, John Deere, and Ray Pride

Design, sleep, LZW data compression, and memory are the processes under scrutiny in the process. The design of the magazine itself tries to make the reader focus on its own production process.

← Psychedelic Box

Student: Barbaros Kayan

Psychedelic Box is a reference to the psychedelic culture of the 1960s. It is presented in a box, which has the same dimensions and square format of vinyl 45 records. I tried to refer to the distortion of human perception by cropping images and using different colors in text blocks in the layout. While creating the magazine, I tried to think like an editor, thinking about the content. When arranging the text, I imitated the positive space created by the composition of the images on the page. By doing so, I managed to build a strong relationship between them.

Breaking the Rules in Interactive Media Design

Yildiz Technical University, Department of Communication Design

ISTANBUL, TURKEY

Class: Multimedia Design Studio 3
Level: Fourth Year
Faculty: Oguzhan Ozcan and
Asim Evren Yantac
Duration of Project: One Semester

PROJECT BRIEF

In this advance design practice class, the students study how to break the rules in interaction design that they learned in their second-year course "Basics in Interaction Design." We give certain design obstacles to the students, to encourage them to find a new way in their creative look while not ignoring basic usability principles. Each year, we present different design obstacles to monitor student efforts in the course of their design education.

PROJECT GOAL

In this project, we forced the students to design an interface for the temporarily disabled (that is, someone who has briefly lost a necessary ability). A disabled user might, for instance, be a restaurant worker who can use only one hand. The goal of this project is to create design solutions that address basic usability principles.

PROJECT OUTCOME

The students are expected to submit a video sketch to demonstrate their persona, design ideas, and interactive system.

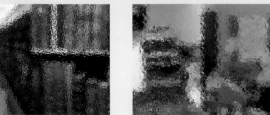

FIELD A   **FIELD B**   **FIELD C**

hall   books   cashier

← **Glossy Interface**

Student: Ahmet Börutecene

The purpose of the study is to apply sound to the interface in a more helpful way. I used filters to distort library images and guide the user to the right menu. Three menus—"cashier," "books," and "hall"—are represented by metaphorical sound icons when the mouse rolls over the related fields. This is a basic example of how auditory icons can be used to navigate an interface. In a secondary study, I didn't use any images, and tried to make the user solve a puzzle through sound.

20

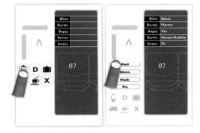

↑ T-Order

Student: Harun Yucesoy

The purpose of this project is to design an interface that is accessible for users with various disabilities caused by environmental conditions. Healthy two-handed persons may be in a situation that prevents them from using one hand. I analyzed the particular circumstances of the targeted users and experienced how to develop a navigation system and design layout that considers the specific conditions and natural obstacles of an environment.

→ Toys under Water

Student: Aybars Pulat

This is a game for children in which four main objects and four complementary objects are to be matched. Some objects are underwater, so the players can't perceive what they are at first. Sound takes on the biggest role in guiding the players to the correct answer. The main idea of this project was to make us think about sound as an element of the interface. This is why I hide some objects from view and use sound to express them. This practice made me realize that sound is an important medium for understanding the interface subconsciously. Especially when there is too much visual media, the use of sound is beneficial.

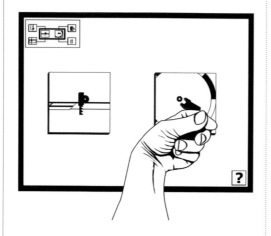

← Touch by Wrist
Student: Özalp Eröz

This project creates an interface for the worker who needs to look at an electronic manual using his wrist because his hand is dirty. The idea is to provide a larger iconic and more flexible layout for using the wrists easily when browsing the manual. A minimalistic graphic style is preferred for an easy look in such working conditions. Comparing a standard interface design problem with extraordinary one allowed me to more deeply understand how a better interactive system should be designed.

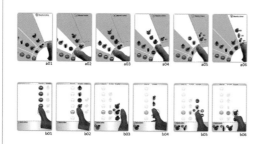

↑ Take Order with One Finger
Student: Turgay Öktem

This project is designed for the waiter who has to take an order using the right-hand thumb because his left hand is full. The main philosophy of the interface layout is based on the finger use located on the bottom-left corner. Interaction is made possible by multitouch drags and clicks. In the beginning, I struggled to set up the design solutions because I was accustomed to website creation following the usual rules. In this project, the condition of the user is unusual. After I rethought the usability rules based on the limitations, I tested myself to ensure that I used the rule for the interface consciously, depending on different user requirements.

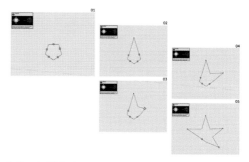

↑ Sonic Painter
Student: Salih Akkemik

It is hard to find creative sound solutions for navigating a two-dimensional interface. There are five dots on the screen that the user should be moving to the right place, which is hidden. I employed a musical piece to express that the user is getting closer to the correct position. As the user drags a point nearer to the correct spot, the number of the instruments in the musical loop increases, so in the end, there is the whole band playing. In another study, I used sonar pulses. These studies made me think of sound as a guiding element of the interface for navigation and resulted in several different solutions for navigational sound without using metaphorical presentations.

Medical Information Design

University IUAV of Venice / Department of Art and Industrial Design

VENICE, ITALY

PROJECT BRIEF

This project is connected to the activities of a research unit in medical design, located inside the Venice hospital. It involves private business firms and research centers giving students first-hand information about the most pressing problems, in order to devise experimental, innovative solutions and to test them under real conditions. The projects presented here deal with different topics in the field of medical information design. One concerns the orientation and information systems within hospital structures, a second concerns the communicative interface of medical products and equipment. Another important subject relates to the distribution and intake of drugs in hospitals and at home. The significance of the communicative aspects in all these cases is heightened by the widespread diffusion of digital technologies and by the changing cultural profile of the users of such information systems.

PROJECT GOAL

The project brief expresses the needs of the different users of information systems as based on previous contacts with various experts and medical institutions. But each student must develop supplementary broad spectrum analyses and interviews, to more thoroughly investigate their topic and to create innovative and unconventional design proposals.

    The project explores different ways to solve relevant social and personal problems by offering the right information at the right time to people needing and providing medical care.

PROJECT OUTCOME

Many of these projects, such as orientation systems for hospitals, electronic clinical records, and vocal and tactile tools for blind people using dispensers, are on the road to being realized.

Class: Master in Medical Design/ Information Design
Level: Masters
Faculty: Medardo Chiapponi
Duration of Project: One Semester plus Thesis

↑ **MyKey, Universal Remote Control for Vending Machines**
Student: Erika Cunico

It's important for vending machines to be accessible to everyone, so they don't create new social barriers. This project analyzes the automatic distribution theme, from food distributors to ticket machines, aiming to increase the use of this technology to make it easily accessible to people with impaired vision. The idea developed in this project is to update existing machines with a new technological device: MyKey, a remote control that communicates with the vending machines using Bluetooth technology. MyKey will tell blind people which kind of vending machines or distributors are they in front of and what services and possibilities each of them offers. Using the remote control and its pad, they will be able to select its functions. During this operation, the person receives audio and physical feedback. For example, a short acoustical sound or a light vibration will help the user identify their choice.

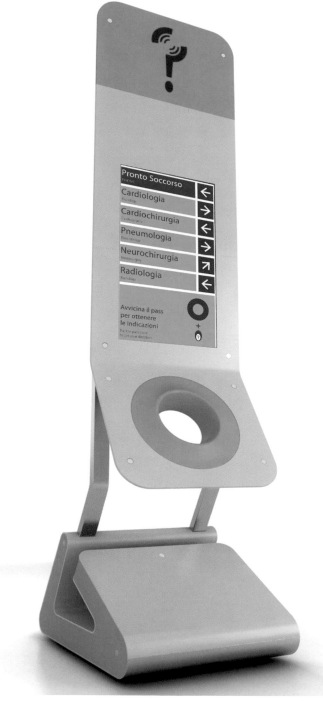

← Smart Wayfinding Totem

Student: Carlo Busolin

The Smart Wayfinding Totem provides a flexible solution to wayfinding in a hospital environment. When one enters a large and complex public space such as a hospital, it is usual to feel out of place and confused. To solve this problem, I imagined providing every hospital visitor with an RFID transponder, tagged with their destination, and leading them there along the shortest path, with the support of "intelligent" totem poles. To achieve this, I designed a dispenser that supplies a tagpass containing an integrated memory and antennas to communicate with other poles, purposely designed to lead guests to their destinations. The poles are fitted with a screen and specific hardware able to exchange information with the RFID card in the pass. When guests bring their pass close to the pole's antenna, hidden inside a yellow shell, the system reads their destination and directs them appropriately with an audio-visual message.

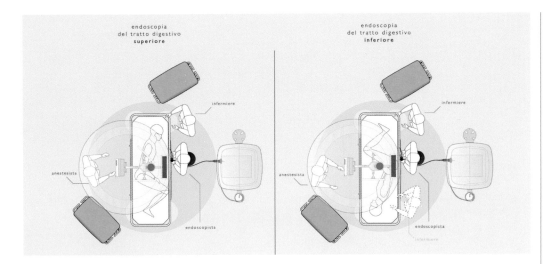

↑ New Configuration in Endoscopy Room Components

Student· Nicolò Luppino

This ergonomic configuration was designed to help doctors better interpret images of the endoscopy without errors. The project is being seriously considered by Padua's hospital.

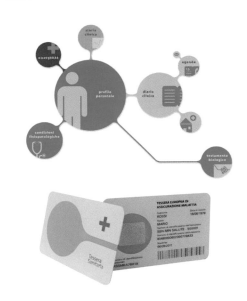

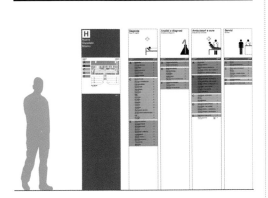

↑ New Mestre Hospital Orientation System

Students: Nicolò Luppino, Carlo Busolin, and Anna Pasini

The goal of this project was to design a simple and clear orientation system.

↑ Molecular Health Records

Students: Nicolò Luppino and Carlo Busolin

The goal of this project was to supply citizens and healthcare operators with an instrument that speaks a friendly language and that can collect the entire clinical history of patients, with the objective of supporting adequate treatments. The project is going to be realized in co-operation with the Bruno Kessler Foundation in Trento, Italy.

Human Rights, Human Wrongs

Massachusetts College of Art and Design

BOSTON, MASSACHUSETTS, USA

22

Class: Poster Design
Level: Junior and Senior Elective
Faculty: Chaz Maviyane-Davies
Duration of Project: Two Weeks

PROJECT BRIEF

The world is in precarious shape and what we manage to do to each other, even worse. "Human Rights, Human Wrongs" is an extremely broad-based theme that allows students to choose and interpret a social issue.

Students will voice their opinions on their chosen issue by creating a visual, conceptual statement for a general audience, using the integration and/or juxtaposition of type and image, possibly in a new or unexpected way. The poster should aim to heighten public awareness of their topic and make viewers question their own beliefs and lifestyles.

How does the effective poster achieve its aim? Remember, by its very nature, the poster has can seize the immediate attention of the viewer, and then retain it for what is usually a brief but intense period. During that span of attention, it can provoke and motivate its audience. It can make the viewer gasp, laugh, reflect, question, assent, protest, recoil, or otherwise react. This is part of the process by which the message is conveyed and, in successful cases, ultimately acted upon. At its most effective, the poster is a dynamic force for change.

The image(s) can be "borrowed" from books or magazines (e.g., photographs and press cuttings), photocopied, rescaled, recombined to create the desired effect, or better still, you can photograph your own imagery. Make sure you credit the photographer. Illustrations have to be your own.

PROJECT GOAL

To explore and express, via images and typography, questions related to the profound effect we have on each other and the environment and to confront the issues that constantly jeopardize the respect for others, thereby encouraging universal values. Remember, fraternity and solidarity are embodied by helping each other and by reciprocity.

→ **Everything Is Bigger in Texas**
Student: John Magnifico

This poster was designed in response to one of the many critical issues surrounding our nation's system of mass incarceration. The state-born slogan "Everything Is Bigger in Texas" represents the misuse of capital punishment. One thing I did not want to do when designing a poster on this controversial issue was to overtly say which side is right and which side is wrong, or pound statistics down viewers' throats. I think it is more effective to send subtle messages that spark people's interest or awareness and let them form their own opinions.

← **Air**
Student:
Damon Jones

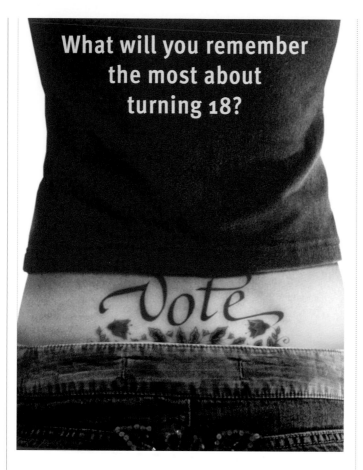

← What Will You Remember
When You Are 18?

What Will You Remember When You Are 18?

Student: Huanwu Zhai

Faculty overview: Speaking to the young about voting can go either way, as apathy pervades a generation with everything. You suddenly find that one thing that seems to matter most in their lives (for now) and turn it around so that they observe and take notice. When this poster was displayed on campus, it seemed that everyone stopped to notice it as they all could relate to it in their own way—the sign of a good communication.

↑ Global Warming?

Student: Daniel de Graaf

This poster calls attention to the notion that solutions are often before our very own eyes. Global warming, although a serious and complicated issue, simply demands a pragmatic investigation and consequent alteration of our habits in order to be reasoned.

→ Let Them Eat Pork

Student: Erin Murphy

This poster was created in response to the French National Assembly's decision to ban Muslim head scarves and other religious symbols from public schools in February of 2004. My response focuses on the ignorance of this archaic decision regarding the traditional practices of Islam, with eighteenth-century Marie Antoinette representing the modern-day French government.

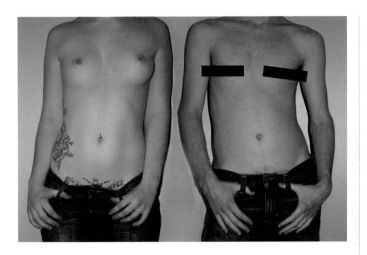

↑ Fashion?

Student: Kaitlin O'Donnell

In a world that is becoming increasingly focused on political correctness, I wanted to bring attention to gender issues. In this poster I have tried to raise questions of true equality between males and females in relation to their roles in sexuality in the media.

↑ Obesity

Student: Stacie Thompson

Here we see that "ah-ha" moment when two completely separate things relate to each other visually and meaningfully and make complete sense.

→ Ride to Save Your Ass

Student: Gabriela Crinigan

I wanted to create a poster promoting bicycle use from a health and/or environmental point of view. I chose to combine both and created an image of clutter and angst to represent our way of life. We are in trouble as the ill effects of technology invade us. Growing pollution calls for physical action over mechanical assistance, and what's better than using, as a way of self-preservation, a man-made object that serves as a proponent of clean air? I chose acrylic on canvas as opposed to digital work since it's pertinent to this nature versus technology battle.

↑ Hidden Child Soldiers

Student: Serena Williams

This poster was designed to raise awareness about child soldiers. As you look closer at the army camouflage print, you can see silhouettes of children at play. The message of the camouflage print is that these children might look like soldiers but are in fact still children. Playing is what they should be doing.

Illustrating a Fiction Spread

Missouri State University, Department of Art and Design

SPRINGFIELD, MISSOURI, USA

23

Class: Image Design
Level: Junior
Faculty: Cedomir Kostovic
Duration of Project: Three Weeks

PROJECT BRIEF

Your task is to produce an illustration for a short story to be published in a fictional magazine and come up with design solution for a spread. Illustration is a visual counterpart to a written text. Successful illustration stimulates the potential reader's imagination enough to make the story worth reading; it suggests what the text is about, it supports it visually, and after the reading, it helps broaden and deepen the reader's intellectual and emotional horizons. In this exercise, we will try to create a multidisciplinary whole. We will put literary content and visual imagery in harmony, so that they support each other in a mutually beneficial relationship.

The full-color double spread you are about to design must incorporate the title, subtitle, and author's name, at least one column of text from the beginning of the story, page numbers, and the name of the magazine. Please carefully read the story to be illustrated more than once; think what could be the most important message it communicates. Be aware that writers often use symbols and metaphors. While reading, write notes, make sketches. Create a large selection of sketches that suggest (not depict) the content of the written text and evoke its mood. Try to find your inspirations through broad research about the time and the place where the story is situated. At a certain point, start thinking about the role of typography in your design solutions. Look at all your sketches, compare them and analyze them critically; select only the ones that

intrigue your imagination and invite you to read the story.

To select the best idea, consider which sketch has the biggest capacity to broaden the reader's scope of thoughts and associations communicated by the text. There are no limitations on the use of media—your choice should be a logical consequence of the formal requirements of your concept. You have to design three solutions targeting three different audiences: hip teens; a conservative crowd; and an upperclass, sophisticated readership.

PROJECT GOAL

The goals are to introduce students to conceptual problem solving; to use research as inspiration and direction toward problem solving; to coordinate accumulated experiences from previous classes (typography, layout design, image making); and to devise successful solutions aimed at a target audience.

↑ **Passion**

Student: Sherri Brown

NAPOLEON WAS IN FULL RETREAT. HE HAD, AFTER SEVEN YEARS OF MARRIAGE, INSISTED UPON SEPARATE BEDROOMS, AND JOSEPHINE'S ENTREATIES TO THE CONTRARY HAD BEEN OF NO AVAIL. As the general's career progressed, great numbers of ladies, many of them young, pretty, and clever, stood willing to divert him. He was six years his wife's junior, and although she still appeared young, having been described by a contemporary as one of those women who "stay at thirty for fifteen years," Josephine felt like one of her own cut flowers, about to be replaced before she had begun to fade. Her stratagems to hold her husband's attention grew increasingly reckless.

Botany was her passion, Bonaparte aside, and in its service she supported some of the most notable gardeners and naturalists on the continent. The gardens of Malmasion, the Bonaparte estate, were already acquisition was

(continued on page 38)

The Dahlia

TREACHERY

By Myrna Davis

THE SUMMER AMERICAN | 24

↑ **Sophisticated**

Student: Tomlinson Jared

Optimism

The Chrysanthemum

By Myrna Davis

It was one of those autumn evenings that come unexpectedly after the first frost, a straggling remainder of summer. Akiko lingered in the moon viewing room, envisioning the features of her beloved on the moon's bright face. Then the clouds drew across it, their edges glinting with reflected light, until she could imagine him no longer. Smoothing her heavy kimono embroidered with the colors of the season, she moved toward the obscured garden.

She did not change into the wooden sandals meant for garden walking, removing instead her white *tabi* and stepping along the path with bare feet, taking pleasure in the feel of the moss, velvety damp with dew. Among the twisted pines and tiny maples, the gentle ginkos with fluttering fan-shaped leaves, the stands of bamboo clicking and rustling in the wind, Akiko brooded about her future.

She still was eager to be married, but only to Takeo. Three times she had seen him, each one a formal occasion. They had behaved correctly, bowing deeply to each other, averting their eyes. But there was a genuine attraction between them, and they gladly acceded to the betrothal sought by their families. After their last meeting, Takeo's image had stayed with her constantly, and often made her feel detached form her surroundings. As she prepared for their wedding, she would recite his name with each small task, with each tiny stitch in her sewing. Takeo, Takeo.

continued on page 43

↑ **Optimism**

Student: Annie DeGraff

↑ **Consolation**

Student: Sarah Jemes

↑ **Hip**

Student: Zender Daniel

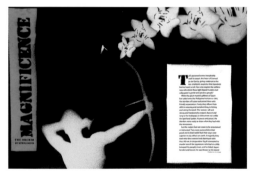

↑ **Sophisticated**

Student: Candis Spraul

↑ Consolation

Student: Abigail Reilly

↑ Wisdom

Student: Jessica Schmidt

↑ Wisdom

Student: Richards Scott

↑ Passion

Student: Dustin Jacobs

↑ Secrecy

Student: Myriam Bloom

↑ Conservative

Student: Steffes Kelsey

Prague Souvenirs

North Carolina State University, College of Design

RALEIGH, NORTH CAROLINA, USA

24

Class: Advanced Graphic Design Studio:
Study in Prague
Level: Junior and Senior
Faculty: Denise Gonzales Crisp
Duration of Project: Three Weeks

PROJECT BRIEF

Design a series of souvenirs that communicates the experience of Prague—artifacts that move beyond. The souvenirs will anticipate what might be meaningful to others. The series can take the form of portable objects, postcard, booklets, T-shirts, etc. Objects may be constructed, prototyped, or visualized in renderings or illustrations.

PROJECT GOAL

The aim was not simply to apply graphics to standard souvenirs, but rather to integrate the object, message, and form into collectible artifacts. Students were introduced to the private and public motivations behind clichés found in current souvenirs through reading, analysis of current souvenirs, and discussion. They were asked to respond to Prague having had real experiences as tourists, by identifying what would be of particular sentimental value but also more meaningful than the average souvenir.

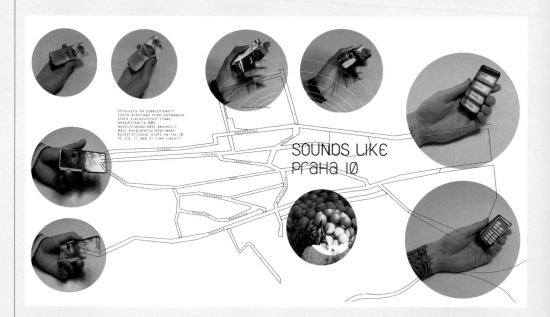

↑ Sounds Like Praha
Student: Sarah Leigh

This hand-held device captures the distinctive sounds of Prague, such as approaching trams.

↑ Prague Boxes

Student: Jeffrey Shroyer

Instead of designing one box that did several impossible things, I designed several boxes with simple, realistic actions. Each box is mechanically driven, no electricity required. The mechanical action creates both the music and motion of the boxes. The boxes are composted of hand-painted tin cutouts. The mechanical parts are assembled by local Czech watchmakers. The boxes are quite small, measuring at most 1 ½ inches (3.5 cm). The boxes come in plastic spheres that are dispensed from gumball-type machines for a fee of five crowns a piece.

The first box contains the syncopator factory powered by Prague's local music man on Charles Bridge. Music from his CD *Super Dance*

Music accompanies all of the boxes in action. The music man tips his hat to passers-by and his little monkey friend flips for joy. Birds fly out from behind the bridge, and his little drum beats to the song.

The second box depicts a typical Czech meal of beef goulash, potato dumplings, and beer. The action of this box is manually driven, a small lever switches the meal between the before and after stages.

The third box displays a phenomenon experienced on the way down to the metro. While on the escalator if a person tilts their head to the side, the other travelers appear to be leaning backward, as if in a strong wind. This illusion is aided by the orientation of advertising aligning with the escalator handrails. The advertisements have been replaced with posters from our first project. The action in this box is manually driven as well. A small lever tilts the escalator back and forth. Too much tilting will cause the passengers to fall. It is a game of sorts.

The final box depicts the crowds in front of Prague's famous astronomical clock. Large groups of people usually gather here to be simultaneously disappointed by the clock's limited hourly action. So the crowd gyrates in anticipation of the event and once it happens they stand still and sigh in disappointment.

← Prague Chandelier Earrings and Packaging

Student: Emily Millette

Everything about Prague is a little quirky and unusual, but somehow the variety of aesthetics works together. After looking through some of my pictures, I realized that ornate light fixtures are a detail of daily life that begins to capture this quirkiness rather effectively. They are striving for refinement, but end up falling a little short of real luxury.

↑ Pivo Coasters

Student: Jaime VanWaart

There are many customs in Prague about drinking, such as how one toasts, drinks, and orders beer. The coasters introduce and document these customs in association with the variety of beer labels originating in Prague.

→ Prague History Chess Set

Student: Nicole Kraieski

I wanted to create a souvenir that was useful and particular to Prague. Of the souvenirs in the markets, the things that I found most engaging are the chess sets, because chess is a game that people of different cultures and language barriers can enjoy. The styles of chess sets seen in the markets in Prague are identical to the ones we saw in Kraków; though their designs are unique, they are particular to a wide range of places in Eastern Europe. My idea was to design a chess set that spoke specifically about Prague and its history. They would be designed less for a visitor of just a few days or a week than the visitor that stays long enough to get a feel for the city. The pieces are to be purchased separately and set against each other. Each speaks to a different time in Czech history. The first two sets are Bohemia and Communist Czechoslovakia. Other sets would include present-day Czech Republic, Prague as a part of the Austro-Hungarian Empire, Prague under German occupation, and so on.

↑ Prague Tokens

Student: Masa Tanaka

These tokens help tourists remember the small joys of accomplishment as they learn to get around in Prague. I've created four different sets of transportation tokens that tourists can collect and place in their Prague booklet. These tokens would be sold in vending machines placed in the respective context. For example, sets of transportation badges will be placed in the metro and tram station so tourists can buy them as they arrive.

Souvenir:
Velvet Revolution Plush

VÁCLAV HAVEL

FACES:

DEMONSTRATORS · VÁCLAV HAVEL · JAN PALACH

BACK:

ORIGINAL ART FROM REVOLUTIONARY POSTERS OF '89

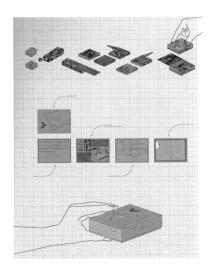

↑ **Ephemera Boxes**

Student: Ioana Balasa

These boxes created of printed ephemera are for tourists to collect organic and other materials from Prague, such as grass, tiny trinkets, dirt, water, and so on.

↑ **Velvet Revolution Dolls**

Student: Kyle Chalk

The clothing for the Velvet Revolution Dolls is to be made of collected materials. The stitching would be exposed, to give a materiality and texture to the fronts of each. There would be consistency in how some of the more specific characters, such as Václav Havel and Jan Palach, would be made into multiples. Ideally, by contrast, the demonstrators would never look the same, which would make for a collective group of all different dolls, with unique personalities. The Revolution was about the masses of people who came together, and by varying the look of each figure, they would begin to echo that important role. The backs would be made of portions of original posters, silk-screened or printed on the fabric. The full poster would be represented on the back of the information card that would accompany each doll. The intent is to represent these characters in a way that would be both inviting to souvenir shoppers and teach them something important about the recent history of Prague and the Czech Republic.

User-Centered Communication

The University of the Arts

PHILADELPHIA, PENNSYLVANIA, USA

Class: User-Centered Communication Design
Workshop
Level: Junior
Faculty: Jorge Frascara and Guillermina Noël
Duration of Project: One Week

PROJECT BRIEF

The workshop involved five projects that addressed the theme of user-centered design, allowing students to experience different ways of involving the user in the design process, including users with special needs. Three students worked on each project.

Several lectures supported the introduction of the projects, discussing user-centered design, visual perception, cognition, design methods, reading theories, and aphasia, as well as planning and executing questionnaires and interviews.

For all five projects, students were required to first analyze the design of the existing information to see how effective it was and how the design could be improved for better user comprehension. Then they were asked to redesign it based on their analysis. The had to consider the design of the new prototype to include information sequence, information chunking, hierarchies, visual strategies to denote hierarchies, memory aids, and details of tone, color, font, and size of type.

Upon completion of the initial design, students interviewed user groups for each project to determine their needs and wants. Using this analysis, students redesigned their prototype and submitted it for review with a one-page report that included a description of the problems and how they arrived at their solution.

PROJECT 1: Medical Information on Nonprescription Drugs for the General Public
This information is normally dictated by legislation and directed to at least three different audiences: physicians, the public, and marketing specialists. Given the amount of information, there is a tendency to use very small type sizes and to crowd as much text as possible in a small space. In a broad sense, every form, every layout expresses and fosters certain cultural values and affects the way in which people deal with things and with other people. The purpose of this project is to find out how a visual communication designer can improve the social and ethical implications while improving the effectiveness of an existing leaflet, through the analysis and reorganization of its content.

PROJECT 2: Diagram Design for Comprehending the Interaction of Traffic-Safety Factors
The structure of verbal language offers limited possibilities to convey information. It promotes linear thinking and is very poor for the presentation of inclusions, simultaneities, multiplicity of kinds and complexity of connections. While all these issues can be described verbally, the nature of the verbal discourse does not reflect the structure of what is being signified. We need to develop thinking strategies that help us understand ecologies of information. Our challenge when attempting to represent a complex problem in a diagrammatic way should not be led by the need to simplify the information presented, but by the need to organize it and present it in such a way where not only could we recognize all the factors that are at play, but also their interactions.

PROJECT 3: Interface Design for an Emergency-Response Web Application

The design of interfaces has been discussed intensely in the last twenty years, and little is to be rescued as universally valid principles. Yet when an interface has a very precise objective, such as it is in our case, serving an emergency-response system, two things happen: one, it becomes more possible to develop design criteria; and two, the success of the interface will be based on very clearly defined task-related performance specifications. An interface of this kind operates more like the control panel of an aircraft than like Google or Amazon. This interface requires training before its use, and each user group has a precise and limited scope. For this project, we should develop a rich-prospect interface design, that is, a home page that displays as much as possible every function and item in the system. The visual presentation affects cognitive facilitation and therefore usability; the usability of an interface affects the users' trust in the service provider.

PROJECT 4: Informing Stroke and Aphasia Patients

Aphasia is a communication disorder. Most aphasia cases are caused by stroke, the sudden interruption of blood flow to the brain. In less than 1 second, the language system developed since early childhood becomes partially or completely damaged. The number of people that suffer from aphasia in the United States has been estimated at about one million. The objective of this project is to design information graphics for people with special needs.

PROJECT 5: Facilitating Reading for Patients with Aphasia

It is quite common for patients with aphasia to suffer some kind of reading impairment. The impairment will differ among individuals, but with clinical assessment some patterns of impairment can be recognized. The objective here is to design a layout that will facilitate reading for people with special needs.

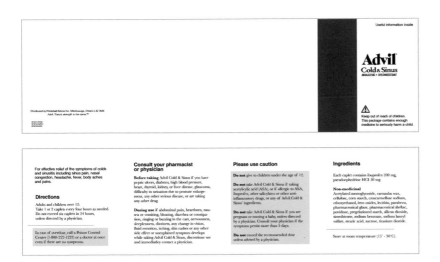

↑ Medical Information on Nonprescription Drugs for the General Public

Students: Greg Deldeo, Jeanette Hodgkins, and Laura Segal

This prototype attempts to emphasize the cautions and warnings by adding a symbol and using a yellow background for the warnings.

The information was reorganized into clearer groups compared to the design in use. The titles were emphasized by increasing the size and intensifying the color.

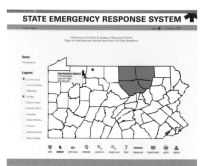

↑ Interface Design for Emergency-Response Web Application

Students: Alexa Falcone and Tim Rinaldi

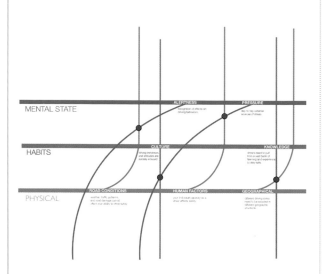

↑ Diagram Design for Comprehending the Interaction of Traffic-Safety Factors

Students: Nichole Bartholomew, Lucia de Sousa, and Milosz Wachowiak

Originally, we were given a terribly confusing chart of twelve categories, all pointing to a circle in the middle that meant all these categories affected driving behavior. Each theme had a few words in bubbles floating around it. There were too many floating bubbles, and it was difficult to figure out where to begin. So the question then became, Should it begin somewhere? The circular shape with all themes pointing to the center obviously did not lead to a starting point. We decided that steps are easier to read. The existing chart had no hierarchy whatsoever, only themes and subthemes. Traffic-safety factors can be narrowed down to two categories: the road user and the environment. The road user refers to the behavior of the users, things that they are in control of and have the power to decide on. The environment refers to the external world, things not within the control of the road user, but elements to be aware of. We removed much of the information from the original chart and added our own. The best way to evaluate the usability of this chart is to ask people if they can read the information and if they want to use it.

The problems we faced were not restricted to creating a user-friendly interface. As designers, we had to imagine how such a program would be set up, especially since none of us had any basic knowledge of programming or databasing. What things could a program do? How complex could you design something that was still understandable? These are the main questions we had to ask at every step. Because we were unfamiliar with programs (and therefore assumed our user might also be unfamiliar), we decided to simplify the entire website to basic terms. The response we got from our users also reaffirmed this belief: all three of our interviewees stressed legibility, simplicity, and clarity of the method of communication. Using the specific feedback we received from our interviews, we created a layout that was quick and to the point. Minimal use of colors helps to illustrate key areas of interest, and additional icons help to stress accessibility at a glance. We took out functions that seemed irrelevant or redundant and kept those that were crucial to navigation and notification. By doing all this, we tried to create a layout that fit our users—a program that was simple and clear in its functionality.

→ Informing Stroke and Aphasia Patients

Students: Josh Hey, Paul Quinn, and Megan Wilde

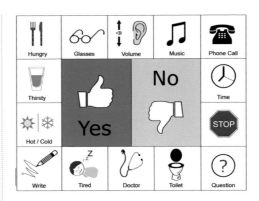

We wanted to create a tool that the doctor could use to explain information to the patient in basic terms. Our first design was based on the articles on aphasia that we were given. We divided the text into five major categories of information. We broke these into five pages and created a layout we thought appropriate for aphasic patients to read. We met with three people affected by different forms of aphasia. Each interview stressed the point that people with aphasia, just coming out of a stroke, strongly desire to interact with people and want information about what has happened to them, not be talked down to or talked over. We had a couple diagrams that we thought of including, but after our interviews, we decided that adding some sort of imagery was imperative. All three interviews stressed the importance o images, because it is difficult to predict which patients will be able to read text and which will not, so accompanying images can bridge the gap in comprehension. The images also can assist the doctor in explaining which areas of the patient's brain and body have been affected. All our interviewees agreed that the size and legibility of our original was good, but they suggested simplifying the text into easier terms. We discovered that eliminating long sentences and isolating key words would make it easier for the patient to understand. Also based on our interviews, we decided to include blank paper at the end to allow the patient some form of expression, as well as a separate sheet with additional resources about aphasia for family members.

← Facilitating Reading for patients with Aphasia

Students: Stephanie Koleda, Daniel Kwon, and Crystal Shepard

Our first imperative was choosing a user-friendly font so that the aphasia patients wouldn't confuse letters such as *b* and *d*, and a lowercase *l* and an uppercase *I*. We selected Century, a serif font, instead of a sans-serif font, since it shows more differences between these letters. For the text size, we needed something that would be large enough for the users to see, since some people with aphasia read the letters as symbols rather than as letters. We needed enough letterspace for those who can read only letter by letter, as well as for those who can read word by word. The spaces between words and lines were important as well, so that readers could see where the words began and ended, and so that enough space existed between the lines for the text not to overwhelm them. We definitely preferred color over black and white since it is more pleasing and still provides contrast. For our prototypes, we considered a poster and a pamphlet. The pamphlet could be read one paragraph at a time. Yet, with our original pamphlet, the horizontal format of the paper and text was a bit of a problem, since text is usually in a vertical format; this is what we used on the poster and it was favored by our interviewees. To satisfy this problem, we combined the two formats.

Creating Meaningful Graphics

Jan Matejko Academy of Fine Arts in Kraków, Faculty of Industrial Design, Department of Visual Communication

KRAKÓW, POLAND

Class: Graphics Studio B
Level: Undergraduate
Faculty: Jan Nuckowski
Duration of Project: One Semester

↓ Graphics for Packaging Medications

Student: Adelina Arendarska

I wanted to design graphics for packaging medications that would be easy for consumers to understand, include multiple tasks, and emphasize safety.

→ Promoting Fair Trade

Student: Maria Korzenska

Aware of the importance of the idea of Fair Trade in the world today and the fact that its existence is relatively unknown in Polish society, I made it the topic of my project. I designed a hypothetical organization doing Fair Trade certification of products and producers and other activities promoting the Fair Trade concept.

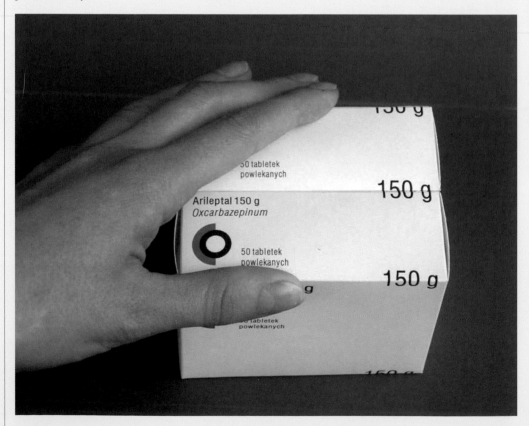

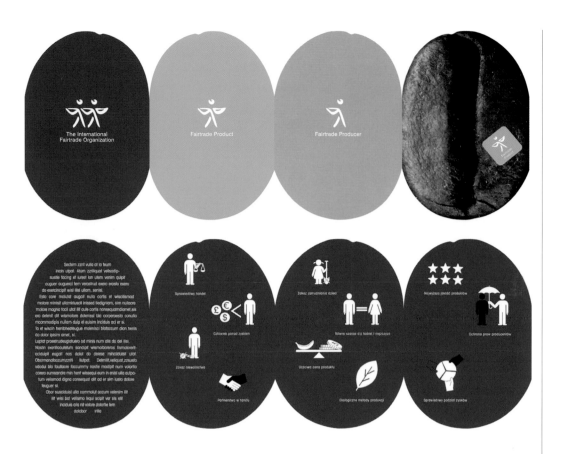

↑ What Are Vitamins and What Do They Give Us?

Student: Olga Chodakowska

These graphics illustrate the benefits of vitamins to the health of the body and demonstrate that complicated information can be conveyed through simple forms.

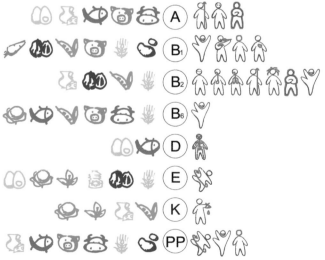

Najważniejsze witaminy, ich wpływ na organizm i produkty je zawierające

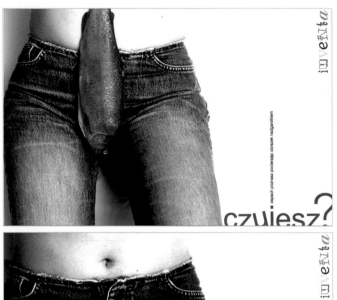

↑ Personal Hygiene Campaign

Student: Karolina Kempa

These dramatic photographs immediately conjure the senses—anyone can understand what's being communicated simply through the image.

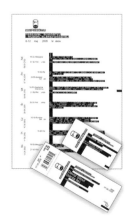

← Music Festival Materials

Student: Dominik Blok

I wanted to create music festival graphics through the simplest means necessary for use in print and on a website.

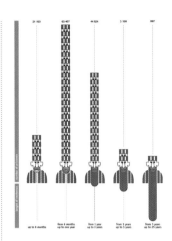

↑ Visualizing Statistical Data

Student: Monika Bielak

Visualization of statistical data is a large and significant aspect of visual communication, but it is often neglected by Polish designers. This chart illustrates the number of people in prison and the duration of their sentences.

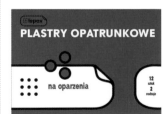

↑ Lepex Package Design

Student: Monika Mlynarczyk-Pacewicz

The concept of packaging should present an adequate semantic leitmotif for the product. The design should also clearly identify the family of packaging and at the same time make it possible to easily identify a particular product.

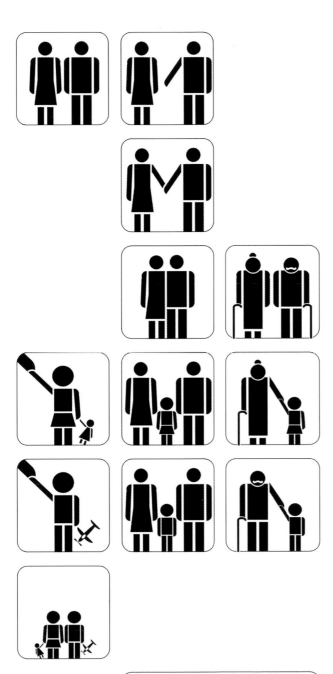

↑ Tax Return Form

Student: Seweryn Puchala

Designing a tax return form is complex and multifaceted. A form should reflect the state's concern for the welfare of its citizens. Citizens, on the other hand, should trust that, first, they are paid decently for their honest work and, second, that their taxes are not embezzled but spent in ways benefiting the common good. Finally, the trust mentioned should be enhanced by the form's design.

← Family Relationships

Student: Szymon Kiwerski

This is an introduction to designing sign systems, showing how signs could denote family relationships.

Make a Chair

Portfolio Center

ATLANTA, GEORGIA, USA

27

Class: Modernism: History, Criticism and Theory
Level: Third to Seventh Quarter
Faculty: Hank Richardson
Duration of Project: Nine Weeks

PROJECT BRIEF

"The primary focus of a chair is you can sit in it, while its secondary function is to embody a set of aesthetics or values, or to communicatea message or opinion. The secondary functionof design is the primary function of art: this is where the two cross over."
—Angus Hyland, Pentagram, London

Portfolio Center's "Modernism: History, Criticism, and Theory" class explores design history and criticism as a catalyst for new ideas. You will be assigned a particular art movement to research. You will then teach that period to your classmates via lively presentations. There is a long tradition of superlative theater in this class; you're expected to carry on that tradition. Next, you will consider how to design a chair within the style and context of the design movement. Most essential to this assignment is that the chair integrates your own unique history and values, thus becoming a metaphor for you as an individual in the world. This involves drawing from private experience and handling subject matter outside your comfort zone. You will discover exactly what you're made of as individuals, as artists, and as revolutionaries, because before these nine weeks are up, you must design, research, and choose materials, create models, and deliver your designs to be built.

PROJECT GOAL

Students are charged with combining the inspiration from a randomly selected artistic movement and a personal experience to create a piece of furniture. Students must see the project through, from conception to fabrication, working closely with the craftsmen who build their chairs. Not only are the resulting chairs beautiful metaphors, but they stand as testament to the passion, commitment, and perseverance of their designers.

← Sister Chair / De Stijl
Student: Rachel Strubinger
Builder: Walt Wittman

→ Impermanence/Futurism

Student: Christy Errico

Builder: Doug Turner

My chair represents change. The seat is supported by a delta, the symbol of change. The shape loosely alludes to the infinity symbol and the idea that change is truly infinite. The cushion is there to provide comfort through change, because no matter how strong we are, a little support during those periods never hurts. Finally, the three dots on either side of the chair represent the three sets of people who have been the only constants in my life besides change: my grandparents, my parents, and my siblings. Remembering that they are there with me somehow, physically or in spirit, helps me to better embrace my journey.

↑ EVO/Futurism

Student: Keith Oh

Builders: Michael Gilmartin, wood;

Andrew Crawford, metal

I moved to the United States from South Korea when I was young, and this chair represents my search for my own voice. The legs represent my roots and are arched to look like a person kneeling. The stripes stand for the influence of Western culture. It doesn't have arms, so you have to push yourself forward to get up. The solid steel piece on top represents my backbone. Five pads represent the different experiences in my life, and the holes in the pads look like cells, to represent growth. Steel gives the chair support but has a heavy weight.

→ Tolerance/Postmodern

Student: Julie Rado

Builder: Doug Turner

Inspired by a conflict that caused me to lose several dear friends I grew up with, this chair is a metaphor for tolerance, or the ability to consider different perspectives. I want viewers to understand that everyone has his or her own truth. Just as there is no "right" way to view anything, there is no "right" way to sit in the chair. It's made for multiple people. Those who sit in it choose to do so; they choose to deal with others sitting with them, shoulder to shoulder and face to face.

↑ One Memory/Basel School

Student: Kevin Scarbrough

Builder: Michael Gilmartin

I was small-town and fourteen years old when we met. I'd just turned eighteen when we found ourselves somewhere in Bryce Canyon at sunrise. There were three weeks and five thousand miles (8,047 km) of road, dust, and sunscreen between us and home. We were broke, hungry, and happy. Time was unimportant and crept by unnoticed. In this freedom, I realized that the only path to happiness is self-governed and self-discovered. This pale, banded wood chair symbolizes humble optimism fortified with experience. The form carefully nestles the body with appropriate support or freedom.

↓ Morris Lounge/Bauhaus

Student: Dave Whitling

Builder: Donald Cope

The Morris Lounge became a metaphor for my journey toward establishing and maintaining independence within my life. The name "Morris" came from an amalgamation of two of the people who have most influenced this journey, my mother and her father. Learning the strength and value that a personal story can lend to a design, regardless of form, is something that I've strived to integrate into much of the work I've done since.

← Self-Doubt/Vorticism

Student: Meggan Wood

Builder: Reed La Plant

The chair embodies a time in my life that was riddled with self-doubt. Sheer boldness and unbridled confidence, symbolized by the orange-threaded plank, have been charred and torn away from the body of the chair, leaving only a remnant of my former self. The rest of the chair takes on a riblike structure with threadbare beige cushioning that indicates a lackluster complacency. The structure as a whole alludes to the remaining shell of a person, with the charred plank serving only as a mocking reminder of the person that once was.

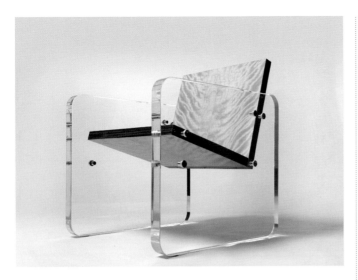

↑ Personae/De Stijl

Student: Mike Kelly
Builder: Walt Wittmann

This chair interprets the values of the De Stijl design movement through the lens of a meaningful personal experience. The bolts in the seat allow it to pivot between two positions that contrast each other dramatically in their level of comfort for the user. The positions represent dual persone in the context of my experience. The angle of the seat and the options for weight distribution inside of a transparent support structure express a point of view that a transformation to self-reliance and, ultimately, happiness is function of transparency and the will to change.

→ Impact/Atomic Style

Student: Dave Werner
Builder: Andrew Crawford

This chair is inspired by the atomic period and by personal experiences on September 11. My father worked at the Pentagon, and for three hours after the attack, I didn't know if he was dead or alive. The form conceptually emulates a plane, with five spires emerging from a central point of impact, symbolizing my diverse emotions upon hearing the news. Sitting in the chair positions the viewer leaning back, looking up toward the sky, with the intention of finding clarity in the middle of these chaotic impulses.

↓ Embrace/Atomic Style

Student: Amanda Babcock
Builders: Michael Gilmartin, wood;
Andrew Crawford, metal

Creating this chair was both terrifying and thrilling and, in retrospect, signifies a real turning point in my life. Being naturally shy, I've always judged myself for not being more outgoing. To cope, I've hidden this turmoil behind a façade of cheerfulness and perfectionism. This chair embodies that struggle: its neatly striated seat is polished, yet something very different struggles to peek out from behind this surface. The metal intertwines with wood, at first appearing out of place. Yet accepting the metal's presence allows its beauty to become apparent and highlights its importance in the success of the overall piece.

Books for Travel

Folkwang University Essen

ESSEN, GERMANY

082

Class: Book Design
Level: Third Year
Faculty: Ralf de Jong
Duration of Project: One Semester

PROJECT BRIEF

Make a concept for a series of books specially designed as travel companions, either for commuters or tourists.

PROJECT GOAL

Specify a target market for your books and determine their wants and needs. Then look at books currently available in the market to see how they can be improved to meet the needs of your market. Pay special attention to how improvements can be made visible to enhance the marketing possibilities. Try to find a balance between innovative detail solutions and the traditional concept of a codex.

↑ Student: Marieke Wüller

I designed a series of books with texts on travel. Geographic images are placed throughout the text, noting every city in its national context. Each book is accompanied by a DVD, allowing viewers to watch the film version on a laptop. Book and DVD are packaged together in a slipcase.

↑ Student: Alexandra Blatt

The paperbacks I usually read on the train get dirty and torn from transporting them in my handbag. I've tried to combine the advantages of a paperback (cheap to produce, small, lightweight) with those of a hardcover (robust, more durable). My book is small (DVD-case-sized) and lightweight (printed on very thin bibleprint). It goes together with a strong but lightweight aluminum box. The box fits all books in the series, so it has to be purchased only once. Each book gets the maximum protection for the minimum price. The typographic arrangement is traditional and economical. The font, Scotch Roman, is rather heavy and very readable even in small sizes—another reason to print only on every second spread.

↑ Student: Pavlina Boneva

I have experimented with innovative materials from the industrial sector to create a cover that offers protection.

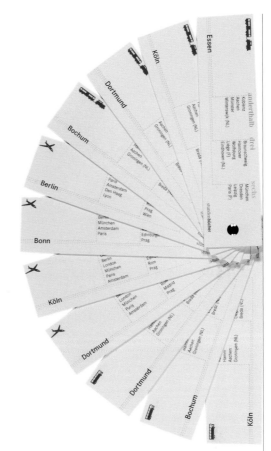

↑ Student: Diana Tessmer

Tourists read more often on the train or plane than at their final destination. Depending on how long it takes to get there, they want to read a short or a long novel, but most certainly, they don't want to finish while still on their way. And neither do they do want to finish their reading with a break of two or three weeks on their way back home. I designed a series of books that all have 160 pages but contain texts of different length. It is the amount of text per page that varies. I have developed three different layouts, working with the three forms of Kurt Weidemann's Corporate typeface: Corporate Antiqua, a (more or less) classicist design; Corporate Sans, a sans-serifed design; and Corporate Egyptienne, a slab-serif design. The sewing and binding of the series is most economical because of the uniform size and number of pages.

↓ Student: Mareike Hundt

I designed a series of bilingual books. Readers can switch to the language of the country they are traveling in by flipping the book over.

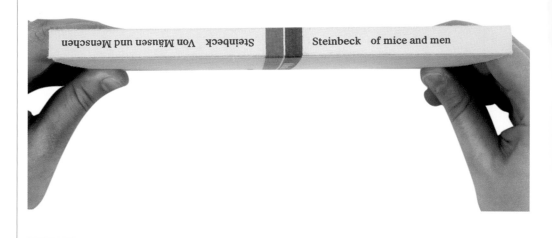

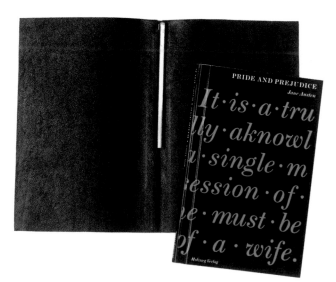

↑ Student: Stefanie Schoenig

I have designed a series of interchangeable leather book jackets with a steel pin that connects the jackets to the books. Now I can read Jane Austen on my trip, and make people believe I'm reading Goethe.

↑ Student: Anna Zaremba

I regard the cover of my book as a stylish accessory. I have designed different wool-fitted covers that have worked-in magnetic strokes. The books come as plain white brochures with the title blind-stamped on them and a band identifying author and title more visibly (for sales support in the store). The binding has magnetic strokes that match up with the covers. The covers are interchangeable and can be applied according to surroundings, personal mood, and such.

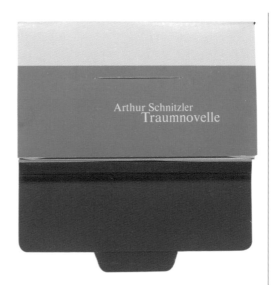

↑ Student: Lea Reck

I designed a book whose cover also serves as a card box. Thus, the book can be read while on holiday and then be sent back home or as a gift to a friend.

↓ Student: Friederike Brandenburg

I designed a series of books for outdoor sporting holidays. They are printed on water-resistant paper (perfect for backpackers). The text size is rather large and ideal for reading under poor conditions. The typesetting is very economical to save weight but there is a space for your thumb to hold the book. The red cover can serve as a help signal in case of emergency.

↑ Student: Juliana Mittmann

I designed interchangeable books and covers. The fashionable covers are upholstered and serve as a cushion on long travels.

Collage Poster Workshop

Rhode Island School of Design

27

Class: Poster Design
Level: Junior, Senior, and Graduate Elective
Faculty: Nancy Skolos
Duration of Project: Three Weeks

PROJECT BRIEF

The creative act of collage can provide end-less inspiration for graphic design students. Everything in a graphic designer's bag of tricks—words, ephemera, materials, colors, and contexts—can be recombined to create unique visual/verbal phenomena. These visual configu-rations engage both our minds and our eyes and challenge our preconceptions. Collage is at once a process and a result. It has been employed for at least a century, and its potential as a creative force shows no sign of being exhausted. As a methodology collage is invaluable. Once a proj-ect is underway in our studio, more often than not, the tossed-aside pile of scraps at the edge of the desktop is far more provocative than the project being "designed."

These unexpected accidents that exist be-hind the scenes, in drawers layered with cut-up colored paper from earlier creative activities, have sparked and sustained our creative energy for decades. In teaching, I have also employed collage to make intuition a more tangible, teach-able experience. This exercise uses thousands of pieces of chopped-up magazines as the cata-lyst for a liberating exercise in how content and form can be negotiated. The fluidity of mixing and stirring up pieces and the resulting happy accidents—contrast, scale shifts, and collisions—releases an uninhibited sense of play.

Materials needed: Black construction pa-per to make a pair of L-shaped framing pieces approximately 8 to 10 inches (20.5 to 25.5 cm) long in each direction. Glue stick and/or clear tape, pencils, a black felt-tipped pen, white pa-per, scissors or X-Acto knife, and tracing paper.

Compositions will be arranged from cut scrap paper. Begin intuitively, sorting through the pile with the framers to see if anything in-teresting seems to be happening. The L's can be focused on a small area or a larger field. Random compositions are framed by the croppers, taped in place, outlined with a pen and trimmed, then glued onto a white sheet of paper. Initially, these should be generated as quickly and with as little calculated thought as possible. Gradually, begin working more intentionally, looking for relation-ships among the scrap pieces like colors and sur-face. Be more deliberate about the alignments as you assemble additional collages. Choose some of your strongest compositions and photocopy them. Observe the difference in the collage as the color is removed and the surface becomes more homogeneous. Keep your favorite com-positions in a sketchbook for future reference. Notice that even if the overall composition is weak, there may be an inspiring detail—perhaps the way a letter is cropped or how a piece of an image meets a piece of type.

PROJECT GOAL

To encounter form and content as malleable; to think beyond your preconceptions to activate space and meaning; to experience the give-and-take of a fluid creative process.

← La Laiterie Events Poster

Student: Hillary Jordan

I created this events poster for La Laiterie, a local cheese-and-wine bistro that offers classes in fine and honest foods. I photographed the cheese in a stark manner to represent the store's "honest" motto, then overlaid a screen of type that says "events & classes." The top layer is a scattering of white signs, alluding to both the typical deli signs and calendar blocks. The large red type is hand drawn, as the bistro's food is handmade. It is meant to contrast the technical san-serif in the white blocks.

← Tim Davis Poster

Student: Sam Gray

The collages that inspired this poster were less about purely formal qualities than about the pairing of images with text (particularly captions) in print and web media. A poster—a public form of information itself—as simply a compilation of other sources of publicity on a certain subject was an approach I hadn't seen before. A viewer might take interest in the poster's content based purely on the fact that its subject (in this case, photographer Tim Davis) is talked about and published elsewhere. Davis's photographs seemed appropriate given his "out of the corner of the eye" aesthetic.

← French Film Poster

Student: Greg Romano

This poster was designed to promote a French Film Festival playing at a local theater. The poster displays both the French and English names of the films as well as the times they play. The composition for the piece is directly inspired by the quick collage made in the first stage of the assignment. The final piece contains remnants of the collage, such as type treatment and overall gesture. Film strips were represented by the large black bars to create a cinematic, monumental gesture. Tracing paper was scanned to create the gradients that I hoped would allude to movie screens. Colors came from the French flag. The entire process was a fluid motion of simplifying and abstracting the initial ideas found in the collage.

↑ Student: Alexandra Mooney

↑ Student: Jay Biethan

↑ Student: Mary-Jo Valentino

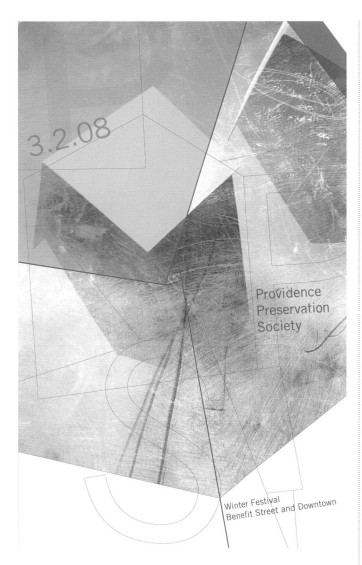

↑ **Providence Preservation Society of Rhode Island Poster**

Student: Seth Clark

In March, the community is invited on a walking tour of the historic buildings of Providence. My hope was to exhibit the feeling of the season along with the historical significance of the buildings on the tour. I made a collage, brought aspects of the collage to the third dimension, and through photography and digital processes created my final solution.

↑ **Gallery Night Providence Poster**

Student: Jennifer West

What was different about this project is that we had to find the topic of our poster from within the collage. To me, the collage resembled many different media—pen marks, calligraphy, paint, charcoal, and photography—contained within a collection of framelike shapes. I decided to make the topic of my poster a gallery. From there, I searched for gallery openings around Providence and found Gallery Night Providence, an event that takes place in many different galleries all over the city and that incorporates all different kinds of artwork. For the poster, I wanted to emphasize the city of Providence as the gallery space instead of highlighting the work of any particular artist. To create the poster, I replicated what I considered to be the most recognizable building on the Providence skyline, building it out of museum board so that it would reflect the white space of the gallery. I incorporated the frames both to reference the collage and to make it feel like a gallery space.

Research Project

RMIT University, The Works, Communication Design

MELBOURNE, VICTORIA, AUSTRALIA

Class: Graphic Design Research (Honors)
Level: Fourth Year
Faculty: Russell Kerr
Duration of Project: One Semester

PROJECT BRIEF

The aim of the research project is to explore a topic of interest and present an informed opinion to an audience of peers. Students present this research in the form of a three to five thousand–word thesis that will also be uploaded to a blog. Below are the project stages.

Formulate a plan: Map out a series of milestones and goals and assign a time frame for each.

Begin the project: Keep visual and written documentation as the project evolves and upload it to the blog regularly. Involve the studio members in regular critiques of the project. Strive to create a unique individual result. Regularly review the progress to ensure the project is in line with the project plan.

Present the project: Students should plan to exhibit their research at the end-of-year exhibition in a format that is accessible to a public audience. The project needs to be presented in both a visual and a written format.

PROJECT GOAL

The research component of the fourth-year honors program is an introduction to postgraduate design research. It utilizes contemporary theories of the role of research in design and encourages critical thinking and dialogue

↑ Packaging Sound

Student: Lee Arkapaw

Music is introduced to us in the womb as a heartbeat. It is the first experience we have of life on Earth. This rhythm is soon accompanied by visuals as we enter the world. From this point on, sound and visuals are intertwined. Can one exist without the other? My explorations into the importance of visually representing sound led me to create my own clip on music creating order.

→ Monstrosity

Student: Beck Haskins

I uncovered a correlation between design, madness, and genius that I dubbed the Madesignius trinity. Monstrosity is a shameless showcase of nonsensical madness that aims to turn the idea of madness into a delightful read rather than a daunting, socially monstrous trait to find in oneself. These traits materialize as forty soft embraceable parts of one's life.

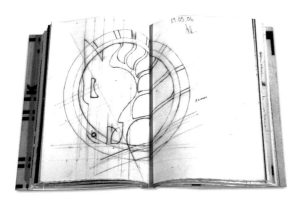

↑ Karasel

Student: David Czech

Ephemeral graphic design for print has always inspired and influenced my approach to visual communication. Karasel is the visual manifestation of printed matter and design thinking.

Undaunted Courage

School of the Art Institute of Chicago

CHICAGO, ILLINOIS, USA

3 1

Class: Advanced Typography
Faculty: Don Pollack
Level: Senior or Graduate
Duration of Project: One Semester

The telling of this historical fiction raises questions about representation as well as truth and the designer's power and responsibility with information. The student must assume three identities in this project: those of the hero, the curator, and the designer.

PROJECT BRIEF

Assuming the role of curator, the student will assemble (and create) a series of historic artifacts. The eras are predetermined and may range from the eighteenth to the twentieth century. Next, a written narrative will be developed that briefly introduces a central protagonist in a story. He or she comes alive through the prose as well as the evidence left behind from the printed ephemera. The documentation includes journals, billheads, personal artifacts, photographs, studies, maps, letters, and invitations. Once the initial artifacts are completed, all of these elements and documents will be designed into a twenty-two-page handmade, hardbound book. This book must be appropriately choreographed to the written narrative and consistent with the character's story.

PROJECT GOAL

This layered novel will also function as a portfolio showcasing all the design basics. Taking inspiration from Renaissance paintings, students will do a series of "master" copies or studies. By exploring historic design through re-creating period artifacts (down to the aged look), the class will address aesthetics and the relationship to technology and culture. The main purpose of this course is to study typography and design history as it relates to our present condition. Typography is a phenomena of our language that is influenced by cultural perspectives—this determines the methods of visual communication and writing systems. Ultimately, the influence of design as a modern media is revealed as a powerful tool of influence in society and culture.

← Undaunted Courage, *The American Frontier*
Student: Salome McCaskill

My project was about a fictional nineteenth-century typesetter living in the Rocky Mountain territory of the American West. The artifact designs were original constructions based on posters, letterheads, and 130-year-old receipts from the special collections of the Chicago Public Library. All of the landscape scenes in the book are original photographs I took from locations in Colorado. This project was a perfect set up for me to further explore the traditions of letterpress and typesetting.

↑ Undaunted Courage,
Jorge Luis Borges's *Garden of Forking Paths*

Student: Mark Addison Smith

I did a visual retelling of Jorge Luis Borges's story *The Garden of Forking Paths*, as a means to understand narrative structure, character development, tone, and typographic nuances rooted within the historical context of World War I. The process began with a critical reading and collage interpretation of Borges's text, set on the eve of the Battle of the Somme when an agent of the German empire assassinates a famous Sinologist to convey the name of a city to be attacked. A visual and typographic breakdown of the story resulted in tangible hand-rendered pieces of "evidence," including aged photographs, passports, teaching certificates, train schedules, and newspapers from the early 1900s, which would become visual examples to accompany the final text. The completed book was case bound, part short story and part exhibition catalog with artifacts.

clockwise from top:

The London Times, Late War Edition, November 13, 1916 (2007), 19.25" × 14" (49 by 35.5 cm)

Passport of Dr. Yu Tsun, 1914, (2007) Photograph of Captain Richard Madden, London, 1915 (2007)

Photograph of entrance to the home of Dr. Stephen Albert

Handmade book, *The Garden of Forking Paths*, by Jorge Luis Borges, 8.25" × 5.25" (21 by 13.5 cm)

MÜNCHEN

1972

OLYMPIC GAMES POSTER, 1972
Munich, Germany

Carlos the Jackal

I WAS SITTING ON SEAT 683. CARLOS WAS NOT IN TIME, FORTUNATELY.

- Page 16 // Line 140

We actually never got the reason why he had to die. The only thing we knew, and that was quite vexing, was that he must somehow have a connection with our intelligence agency. However, we just got our orders and we didn't ask why. But I never forgot this incident and it is still depressing for me to think about it. In fact, killing traitors is really a sign of weakness.

By the late 1970s, the ministry and my department were involved in a number of alliances with forces that used terror as a tactic: the Palestine Liberation Organization, the freelance Venezuelan terrorist and assassin Ilyich Ramírez Sánchez (ironically named after none other than Lenin) who was known as Carlos the Jackal. I met Carlos the first time in 1976. Our meeting was arranged by a friend of mine who believed that Carlos could be valuable for our agency. I had little information about him, so I was unsure if it was a good idea to induct him in our secrets. But in the fifties, the Bulgarians and Poles had the reputation of being the most deadly services. And now 15 years later it was still the same. Our spies where not used to exert violence. But gradually our rivals started to act more aggressive against us. Carlos was used to work under such circumstances.

The Winter Olympics in Innsbruck, Austria, in 1976 provided good cover for a meeting. I was sitting in the stadium on seat 683. It was a sunny day and the atmosphere was excellent. Carlos was not in time, fortunately. I was glad that I could enjoy the contest in the stadium. During this time our agency was in a critical situation, which pushed all of us under pressure. I enjoyed to leave Berlin to spend a day in peaceful München.

CARLOS THE JACKAL, 1977
Munich, Germany

← **Undaunted Courage,**
The Secret Life of 008

Student: K. J. Kim

I designed and wrote about a fictional intelligence officer working during the 1970s Cold War era. She was based on the autobiography of Markus Wolf, the chief of security of East Germany, and her cover alias was that of a stage actress. Designing my book in the format of a theatrical script, I created print ephemera, period piece designs that have encrypted codes and messages between fictional agents.

← **Undaunted Courage,** *The Secret Life of 008*

Student: Christian Eggenberger

This project originated during my exchange semester at the School of the Art Institute of Chicago. I came from Switzerland, and this was my most memorable school experience in Chicago. The project followed a very different path of conception and construction than I had previously experienced. In the end, it was amazing to bring all the prepared artifacts together to create a handmade book about a Cold War spy. I laid it out with four parallel stories told simultaneously.

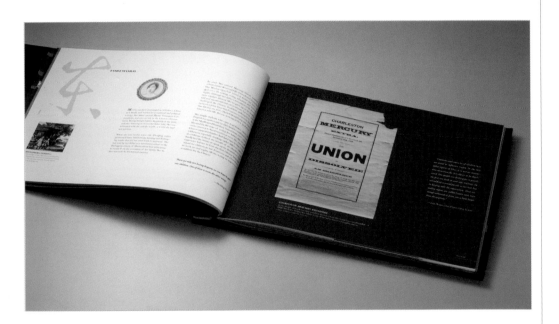

↑ **Undaunted Courage, The American Frontier—In-Between**

Student: Yifen Liu

This book was written in Chinese and English about an immigrant, Mei Lin. The story began at the outbreak of the American Civil War in 1861. I studied historical documents of the late nineteenth century in the United States and China. My goal was to find a personal connection to the lives of early Chinese immigrants in America and to study the issues of a cultural diaspora as well as gender and identity in the increasingly globalized world of the late nineteenth century. As a foreign student from Taiwan, I could connect to the issues surrounding identity by creating a fictional immigrant character. I could relate to my own complex history of coming from Taiwan and having to adjust to a new land. My aim was to explore these issues through the life of a Chinese woman at a specific time and place. This particular research project shed new light on the unique power of design, in that I might be able to help others by giving voice to the major issues of a society. By exploring the methodology of this project, I could consider this as an approach for investigating the role of China in the evolution of Taiwan's complex historical background.

Development of Type Families for Magazines

Senac University Center, Santo Amaro Campus

SÃO PAULO, BRAZIL

32

Class: Project: Design & Visual Communication
Level: Second Semester
Faculty: Priscila Lena Farias with
Delfim Cesário Jr., and José Alves Oliveira
Duration of Project: Eight Weeks

PROJECT BRIEF

Faculty will choose up to five different real Brazilian magazines (for instance, one sports magazine, one children's magazine, one music magazine, etc). Students will be organized into groups of eight to ten members, with each group assigned one magazine. Teams must analyze the typography adopted by their assigned magazine and propose new type families to be adopted in specific parts or sections (for instance, sections titles, article titles, tables, text, captions). Smaller teams will be formed, according to the group overall proposal. Each student in a team is to be responsible for a style (for instance, roman, italic, or bold) within a type family that is the team's responsibility (for instance, a text typeface). The final project presentation will include the design magazine spreads (following the original magazine grid, text, and images), showing the combined use of all typefaces developed by the group.

PROJECT GOAL

Develop typefaces that are not only original, but also technically and aesthetically sound, as well as coherent with the editorial aspects of a given magazine. These typefaces must work well in the context of a type family, and all type families must work well in the context of the magazine spreads.

PROJECT OUTCOME

Develop digital type families.

↑ **Caramella Italic**
Student: Leandro Quaresma

ABCÇDEFGH
IJKLMNOPQ
RSTUVWXYZ
abcçdefghij
klmnopqrst
uvwxyz
0123456789

rinozeronta
regular

ABCYZ
abcyz
01234

17 pt

Feliz Wanderley teve overdose de coxinhas por querer cuçar se junto ao kerning. Rnm, muito

24 pt

Feliz Wanderley teve overdose de coxinhas por

36 pt

Feliz Wanderley teve overdose

↑ **Rinozeronta Regular**

Student: Caroline Ohashi

Rinozeronta Italic designed by Frederico Zarnauskas

↑ **Rinozeronta Bold**

Student: Jasmina Droz

Rinozeronta was developed as a text face for the "Entre-vistão" (big interview) section of the Brazilian MTV magazine. It has a square silhouette that combines with a more organic curve. The final result is not very readable for long texts, and it seems to be more appropriate for titles. The typeface is being used for academic and personal applications.

ABCDEVXYZ
abcdefgtuvwxyz
0123456789

ABCÇDEFGHIJKLMNOPQRSTUVWXYZ
abcçdefghijklmnopqrstuvwxyz
01234567890
.,;:-_—@#$?&*'?/0""''!?¡¿`´¨^~
ÀÁÄÂÃÈÉËÎÍÏÎ
ÒÓÖÔÕÙÚÜÛÑ

← **Caramella Regular**

Student: Rômulo Castilho de Freitas

Caramella is a text face for the Brazilian version of *Scientific American* magazine. The challenge was to develop a text face for a magazine that is well known in Brazil and abroad. The proposal is a serifed face that is light, modern, elegant, and economic. In comparison with the typeface currently used by the magazine, Caramella saves around 10 to 20 percent of text space. The typeface is distributed for free at dafont.com and has had more than 70,000 downloads since November 2006.

zebras caolhas de java querem mandar fax para moça gigante de new york.

ABCCDEFGHIJKLMNOPQRSTUVWXYZ
abccdefghijklmnopqrstuvwxyz
01234567890
.,:;-_—@#$%£*' /()""'''!?¡¿`´^~
ÀÁÂÃÄÉÈÊÍÌÎÏ
ÒÓÔÕÙÚÛÜÑ
àáâãäéèêëíìîï
òóôõùúûüñ

↑ Vazari Sans Regular

Student: Marcela C. Santaella Mamede

Vazari Sans Bold designed by Irina Serrano

zebras caolhas de java querem mandar fax para moça gigante de new york.

zebras caolhas de java querem mandar fax para moça gigante de new york.

zebras caolhas de java querem mandar fax para moça gigante de new york.

↑ Vazari Sans Italic

Student: Felipe Zveibil Fisman

Vazari was developed as a display face to be used in the titles of articles in *Quatro Rodas*, a Brazilian magazine about cars. It is masculine and dynamic, employing a reduced number of curves and inclined lines that suggest movement. The italic and bold versions were developed for use in text boxes with technical information. Letters in the italic version have traditional structures and prolonged terminals.

Adondis Regular

zebras caolhas de java
fax para moça gigante

↑ Adondis Regular

Student: Eduardo Shiota Yasuda
Adondis Italic designed by Natasha Weissbom; Adondis Bold designed by Claudia Crescenti; Adondis Bold Italic designed by Maira Tonietti

Adondis is a text face created for *Quatro Rodas*. It intends to substitute the serifed face currently used, which was considered to have little personality.

Adondis Condensada

ABCÇDEFGHIJKLMNOPQRS
TUVWXYZabcçdefghijklmn
opqrstuvwxyz01234567890.
,;:-_−@#$%&*‴/()""''!?¡¿?˜
ÀÁÄÂÃÈÉÊÈÌÍÏÒÓÖÔÕÙÚÜÛ
Ñàáäâãèéêèìíïïòóöôõùúüûñ

↑ Adondis Condensed

Student: Clara Piochi

Adondis Condensed is part of a family created for *Quatro Rodas*. The condensed version is intended to be used in the price tables published by the magazine. For this reason, its numerals are aligned, unlike the numerals in the other styles of this family.

↑ **Scientific Dingbats**

Student: Bruno Okada

Scientific Dingbats is a font developed for the Brazilian version of *Scientific American* magazine. It has a modern, serious, and direct visual aspect. Some of the pictograms were created to identify the magazine sections, and others are intended to be used in diagrams and graphics.

↑ **Rock 'n' Rock**

Student: Ciro da Cunha Jarjura

Rock 'n' Rock is a display face developed for a section of *Revista MTV* titled "Sub," that focuses on new and independent rock bands. It intends to capture the raw and primitive aspect of these bands' sound and visual communication.

↑ **Ellephont Bold**

Student: Daniela Liquieri

Ellephont was developed as a title face for the Brazilian version of *Elle* magazine. It is light, organized, and clean, but also classy. Ellephont Light designed by Claudia Ikari

↑ **Emme 13 Regular**

Students: Lucas Yasuhiro Momosaki, Juliana Suzuki, and Gabriel Rodriques

Emme 13 is a text family for the Brazilian version of *Elle* magazine. It is light, joyful, and dynamic. Emme 13 Italic designed by Gabriel Pereira; Emme 13 Bold designed by Juliana Suzuki

Type as Metaphor

State University of New York, Purchase College, School of Art and Design

Purchase, New York, USA

PROJECT BRIEF

Each student is asked to research a subject of their choosing. Working with one to three primary texts, they develop four printed panels of any dimension that approach typography as metaphor. The first panel is composed of paragraphs, sentences, phrases. The second panel is individual words. The third panel contains syllables. The last panel has individual letters. Employing research and writing skills, critical thinking, mindmapping, and experimentation, students give form to metaphoric connotations they discover within their text, through compositional arrangement, juxtaposition, and typographic manipulation. Placing particular emphasis on the research process and text analysis, students use a lateral approach, trying many possibilities before refining their four-panel solutions. While we embrace

Class: Advanced Typography
Level: Junior
Faculty: Warren Lehrer and Robin Lynch
Duration of Project: Four Weeks

technology, we discourage the use of filters and other instantaneous computer bells and whistles, and encourage combining handwork with the computer, as well venturing into the physical worlds of the subject matter.

PROJECT GOAL

This project can help design students see type as image, bridge meaning with form, and go beyond utilitarian, overliteral, or preordained approaches to typography.

← Dementia

Student: Hidetoshi Takahashi

Dementia is an illness that affects the brain and memory, making you gradually lose the ability to think and behave normally. I want these panels to be a typo-cinematic portrayal of the fear, anxiety, and sadness, particularly of Alzheimer's. The deep indigo background expresses fear of the illness. The blue type represents the symptoms of the condition—memories, thoughts, and feelings puzzling, fading. The orange type represents the patient's hope, bright but diminishing. The love and voices of family and supporters generate light against the darkness of a bifurcated machine losing its power. September 21 is World Alzheimer's Day.

← Selacaphobia

Student: Chaya Herman

These panels attempt to convey the terror and anxiety that go through the minds of people afflicted with selachophobia—the abnormal and persistent fear of sharks. The first panel describes the condition. The second panel uses the words *shark*, *swimmer*, and *water* to set the stage for the anxiety the swimmer experiences fearing a shark lurking beneath the surface of the water. The third panel uses the word *monster* to build the image of the shark and then the words *torture*, *agony*, *woe*, *shred*, and *pain* to build the teeth signifying where the physical and psychological torment takes place. Lastly, the word *water* (now turning red) is used to visualize the gruesome attack of the victim. The fourth panel uses the letter *S* (for shark) to create the image of bloody water showing all that is left of the victim after the shark has attacked.

↑ Battery Cages

Student: Brandon Campbell

The copy in panel one describes the gruesome conditions of egg farms. The type is stacked and distressed, representing the claustrophobic nature of the hen cages. In panel two, a "debeaked" *K* illustrates the process of beak removal in factory farms. Using only syllables in panel three, the letterforms are further mutilated and crowded into a contained space. The suffix "ing' is repeated, representing a constant flow of eggs below the caged hens. Panel four zooms out, revealing a graveyard of disfigured letterforms. The dying forms rest atop mounds of their product, the way a mother hen tends to her nest.

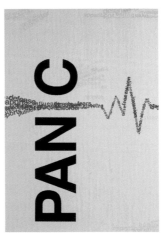

↑ Dyslexia

Student: Marianna Capomolla

Dyslexia is a condition that is far more complex than the stereotypical notion of reading backward. In my panels, I wanted to portray the emotion as well as the learning process that a person with dyslexia struggles with on a day-to-day basis. In panel one, parts of words pop, rotate, and split, portraying how a person with dyslexia reads. Panel two connotes how language can bombard the senses causing confusion. In panel three, individual letters and parts of words remain silent. In the last panel, I tried to convey the loneliness of feeling like something is wrong with you, and then a prideful confidence in knowing that so many others have done well and thrived with the same learning disability.

↑ Mass Hysteria

Student: Cortney Rozell

For my panels, I needed to convey a sense of panic and fear. I tried to portray the way it spreads and grows and becomes something like an infection. The color scheme was very important, as it had to evoke a sense of uneasiness without actually turning people off. I tried to keep the colors simple, reminiscent of old propaganda posters from Word War II.

Horsepower

School of Visual Arts

NEW YORK, NEW YORK, USA

34

Class: Three-Dimensional Design
Level: Third and Fourth Year
Faculty: Kevin O'Callaghan
Duration of Project: Three Weeks

PROJECT BRIEF

Imagine if the world ran out of oil and we were forced to go "full circle" and reinvent existing horse-drawn vehicles to fit into today's environment. Fourteen antique carriages and sleighs were found in barns and fields and transported to a workshop for the students to work on. The vehicles, all in unrestorable condition, were randomly given to the students to make functional for contemporary use.

PROJECT GOAL

An exhibition that creates a satirical answer to today's oil crisis

PROJECT OUTCOME

The traveling exhibition has already been on display at three venues in less than a year, including a Smithsonian-affiliated museum, and has been featured in several national publications. It will continue to grow and tour as new pieces are created and more venues become interested. The exhibition declares, "Imagine a world without oil as a source of power!" Well before the twentieth century, the world depended on another source of power, the horse. The avenues of New York and Main Streets across America were once crowded with horse-drawn vehicles. SVA students have reinvented these vehicles to take on today's energy-challenged world.

↑ Hot Rod Sleigh
Teacher: Kevin O'Callaghan
Photography by MYKO

This was the original starting point for the exhibition.

↑ **New York City Taxi Wagon**

Student: Sofia Limpontoudi
Photograph by Laura Yeffeth

I wanted to re-create the iconic New York City taxicab as a horse-drawn vehicle.

← **Bobbleman's Sales Carriage**

Student: Chris Dimino
Photograph by Laura Yeffeth

This traveling salesman's vehicle sells bobbleheads of the former CEOs of the major oil companies.

↑ Coffee Cart

Student: Alexis Shields

Photograph: Laura Yeffeth

I transformed a disheveled, broken-down sleigh into a sleek, functional New York City bagel and coffee cart.

↑ Ice Cream Wagon

Students: Kaori Sakai & Rafael Vasquez

Photograph: Laura Yeffeth

We wanted to make a whimsical ice cream truck and give a new life to this very utilitarian vehicle.

↑ Con Ed Energy Wagon

Student: Joseph Pastor

Photograph: Laura Yeffeth

I created a perpetual machine that is pulled by a horse and produces energy from horse manure.

↑ New York City Tourist Wagon

Student: Su Hyun Kim
Photograph: Laura Yeffeth

I wanted to pay homage to the New York City tourist bus because it was the first thing I did when I came to New York from Korea. I worked with the design of the original wagon and added to it to create a functional tourist bus.

↑ FedEx Wagon

Student: Sarah Nguyen
Photograph: Laura Yeffeth

In our culture, we try to expedite any kind of process. If we had to go back to delivering with horse-drawn carriages, shipping services would lack dependability and punctuality. Tight deadlines would have to be rethought, Christmas shopping would have to start earlier, and patience would have to be instilled in everyone. FedEx would be forced to change its slogan to "the world almost on time."

↑ Tiki Sleigh

Student: Adria Ingegneri
Photograph: Laura Yeffeth

I retrofit a doctor's sleigh into a "tiki sleigh," while maintaining the original craftsmanship of the existing sleigh.

← Lucky's Brooklyn Pizza Delivery Carriage

Students: Exhibition Team
Photograph: Laura Yeffeth

The purpose was to restore a beautiful carriage to its former glory and to take advantage of its interior space by retrofitting it as a vehicle for delivering pizza.

What Happened?

School of Visual Arts, MFA Designer as Author

NEW YORK, NEW YORK, USA

3 5

Class: Explaining Yourself
Level: Masters
Faculty: Scott Stowell
Duration of Project: Four Weeks

PROJECT BRIEF

This assignment combines traditional information design with more personal subject matter to explore the relationship between who is talking and who is listening—which is, of course, part of every design project.

Select a period of time from your life in which you were involved in a series of events. The time period and the events are up to you.

The idea is to explore how to tell that story on a single surface, and how personal information can be shaped by using a public graphic language. Both the period of time covered and the events that occurred within it should be evident in the design.

Use type and graphic elements only. No decorative or illustrative type, no photographs or illustrations of any kind. Work within these constraints to create something unexpected that nevertheless communicates the facts.

PROJECT GOAL

Examine the relationship between the storyteller and the receiver.

The Blue Period.

↑ The Blue Period

Student: Steven Smith

"The Blue Period" is what my mother calls my first postcollegiate year, in which I moved to New York City with two friends who promptly became sworn enemies, tried and failed to secure dignified employment, and nurtured my inner Holden Caulfield. Over the course of few highs and myriad lows, I wrote at length in a blog. Above, my temperament is plotted via negative words, positive words, and neutral words. Each word is scaled according to the frequency of use in a given month. Blog comments from friends and strangers provide a hint of the support network that helped pull me out of my sea of self-loathing. I struggled to find an appropriate subject matter for this assignment. While I had a lot of rich, detailed data, I don't think my solution was particularly original and I'm not pleased with the result.

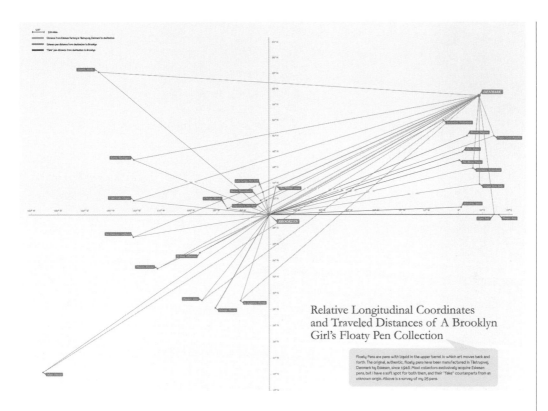

Relative Longitudinal Coordinates
and Traveled Distances of A Brooklyn
Girl's Floaty Pen Collection

Floaty Pens are pens with liquid in the upper barrel in which art moves back and forth. The original, authentic, floaty pens have been manufactured in Tåstrupvej, Denmark by Eskesen, since 1946. Most collectors exclusively acquire Eskesen pens, but I have a soft spot for both them, and their "fake" counterparts from an unknown origin. Above is a survey of my 25 pens.

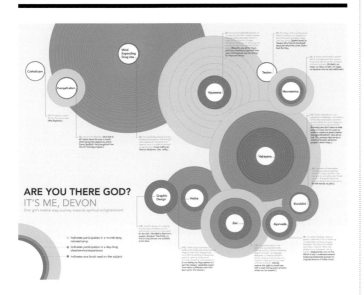

↑ **Are You There God? It's Me, Devon**

Student: Devon Kinch

One girl's twelve-step journey to spiritual enlightenment

↑ **Girl's Floaty Pen Collection**

Student: Lesley Weiner

Floaty pens have colored liquid in the upper barrel that moves back and forth. The original, authentic floaty pens have been manufactured in Tåstrupvej, Denmark, by Eskesen, since 1946. Most collectors exclusively acquire Eskesen pens, but I have a soft spot for both them and their "fake" counterparts of unknown origin. The poster is a survey of my twenty-five pens. In the end, this chart was a scientific approach to a very nonscientific collection. I was really pleased at how I extracted visual and somewhat mathematical data from these treasured objects.

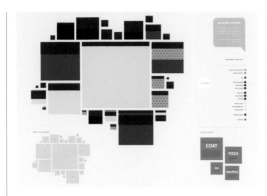

↑ Dad Wants To Know!

Student: Gustavo Garcia

In August of 2007, I moved to New York City from Brazil. In an effort to keep my spending habits in check, my father asked me to keep track of all my expenses for an entire month. This chart represents my spending for November 2007.

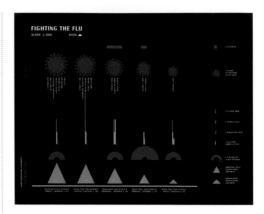

↑ Fighting the Flu

Student: David Ricart

During the time when this assignment was given to me, I came down with the flu. The whole experience felt like a small internal war, and it reminded me of the much-beloved game I used to play as a kid: Space Invaders!

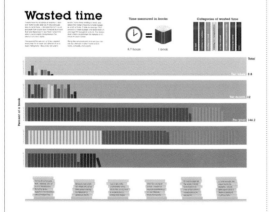

↑ Wasted Time

Student: Steve Haslip

I waste time for all kinds of reasons. I also buy many books and fail to find enough time to read them. I decided that if I could measure how much time I wasted in a form that was important to me, then I would could more easily comprehend the amount of time I waste.

↑ Tattoo Revelations

Student: Jane Song

Tattoo Revelations graphically depicts the unveiling of my tattoos to my immediate family and their emotional responses. I chose the topic because my family is generally conservative and especially toward tattoos.

FACEBOOK WORDS SPECTRUM

JUNE 17, 2007 — JANUARY 31, 2008

This is a chart depicting Facebook interactions between me and my friends during the above dates. Each bar represents a message or a wall post, and the thickness determines the number of words exchanged within them.

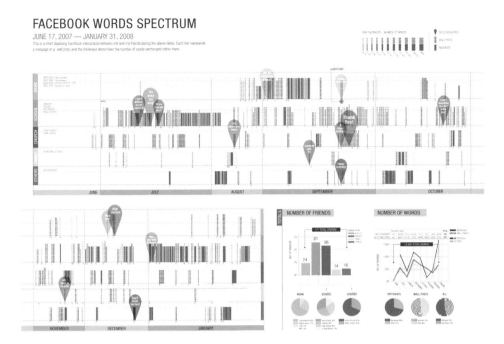

↑ Facebook Words Spectrum

Student: Jia Chen

This chart is a documentation of message and wall-post interactions between me and my Facebook friends. Each bar on the chart represents a message or a wall post, and the thickness determines the number of words exchanged within them. From this chart, I realized that I interact with my school friends, past and present, more than with any other group of friends.

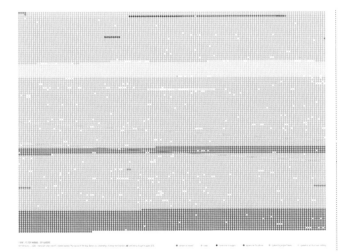

← 1 day: 17,736 words: 341 laughs

Student: Kimiyo Nakatsui

On February 1, 2008, I recorded every sound I uttered over a twenty-four-hour period. After transcribing the audio files and categorizing each word and laugh by type, I created this chronology of my day. Each solid circle represents one word, each outlined circle represents one laugh, and each color corresponds to a category of expression (sung, spoken, laughed to strangers, myself, people I know, etc.).

→ Shower Snooze

Student: Areej Khan

For as long as I can remember, I have had a habit of taking a nap after my morning shower. Experience taught me that the amount of time I spend snoozing affects what my hair looks like when I finally get up. This information graphic charts all possible outcomes and contributing factors to the state of my mane.

→ How Activities and Weather Affect My Hydration: 1 Week

Student: Yaijung Chang

I recorded my hydration for seven days to see how it is affected by my activities and by the weather. I drank water mostly while working and sleeping. I drank twenty-six bottles of water, three tall cups of coffee, three cans of soda, and one glass of wine in just one week.

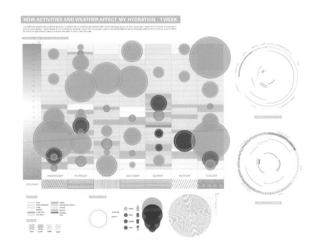

→ A Peculiar Relationship with Water

Student: Jason Bishop

I set out to establish a better knowledge of my hydration habits tracking the types and amounts of liquids I drink and the effect they have on my body's liquid output. My efforts revealed that I rarely drink the suggested daily amount of water, and due to this low intake I had a very low and dark-colored output.

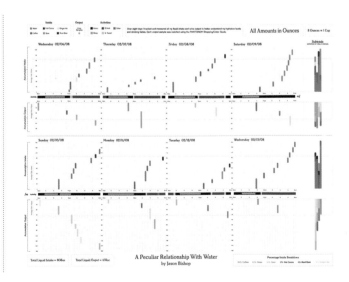

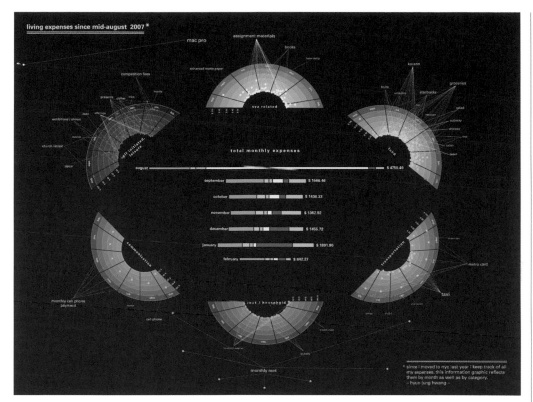

↑ Living Expenses

Student: Hyun-Jung Hwang

Since I moved to the United States in August 2007, I have kept every single receipt. This information graphic reflects my expenses by month as well as by category.

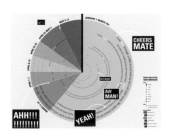

♦My Study Abroad

Student: Kristina Critchlow

This graphic explains my relationships with the people I met during my study abroad.

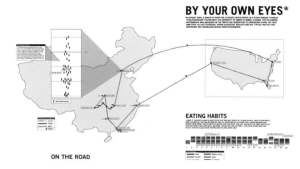

↑ By Your Own Eyes

Student: Nicole Marinake

I wanted to illustrate all the strange things I discovered from leafing through the journal I kept while in China.

Think: The Credibility of Information in the Digital Age

Swinburne University of Technology, Faculty of Design

PRAHRAN, VICTORIA, AUSTRALIA

Class: Design Research Studio:
User-centered Design
Level: Bachelor of Design Honors
Faculty: Nicki Wragg and Keith Robertson
Duration of Project: One Semester

PROJECT BRIEF

User-centered design turns the master/apprentice model on its head and argues that if a design doesn't work for the user, it has no communicative value. We have chosen four main research areas, which students will be asked to investigate from a gendered viewpoint. The research areas are safe sex, drugs, work, and corporatization. The research should start from a gendered point of view but may change to incorporate both genders in the application of research to a specific project. The whole semester will be conducted in mixed communication and multimedia design teams. The brief will evolve over the semester through a number of stages:

Research phase, 20 percent: Students will be allocated to a group and be given a general topic to research and develop into a poster to be presented to the class in week three.

Proposal/user profile and research phase, 30 percent: After week three, groups will re-form and explore their research topics using at least three of the following research methods: literature review, statistical gathering, observation, focus groups, questionnaires, visual analysis, and interviews. These findings will be summarized and used as an argument to support the writing of a proposal brief for each group.

Production and user testing phase, 50 percent: This phase is about applying knowledge and research to produce a multifaceted campaign addressing any special aspect, or issue isolated in a particular topic area. User testing

will occur in week ten so that modifications can take place before presentation in week twelve. Each group will also present a team process journal documenting the path through the various stages of this project.

PROJECT GOAL

At the completion, students will better understand the fundamental philosophy and principles of user-centered design. They will be able to reference literature or design content and construct a user profile from research findings, observation, focus groups, and the experience that informs the development of the proposal. Students will further develop user-centered methods to test and evaluate process and outcomes and employ user research methods to clarify the user's needs, considering issues such as aesthetics, legibility, and usability. Lastly, students will apply information design principles to a practical design outcome in media appropriate to the research problem.

PROJECT OUTCOME

Technology has fundamentally changed the nature of our communication and information seeking. It is the age of blogs, wikis, social networking sites, podcasting, message boards, email, and whatever communication technologies may emerge tomorrow. The basis of this project, undertaken as part of an honors research class with an emphasis on user-centered design, is a simple question: Are we really more informed? The issue focuses on the relationship between the large amount of information available and the level to which we are actually informed. Some questions: How do we determine fact from fiction, right from wrong, good from bad, up from down? In an online environment where information is presented seamlessly, the convergence of information genres can leave it difficult to know what to take as fact or fiction. This project was a unique opportunity to examine how this age of information benefits and detracts from society. Through the development of an online blog, and a series of posters, advertisements, stickers, and postcards, we aimed to generate thought and dialogue about the credibility of online information and, in turn, provide a skill set with which to achieve a higher level of processing information. The aim is to get people to think, to consider, and to question the information that is presented to them so they become better informed.

Think

Students: Meg Phillips, Mary Nelson-Parker, and Emma Woods

Posters directing how and where to blog were placed in key positions around computers and technology, within universities and libraries. Based on creating awareness and a thought pattern when processing information, the aim is to get people to consider and question everything.

A blog site was developed as a central part of the project, aimed to promote a discourse of information credibility online. The blog itself represents the core of our project, the space in which the dialogue we hoped to create takes place. The posts are generating thought and prompting a discourse.

Postcards left around universities and libraries act as a reminder of the project's aim.

Magazine advertising also plays on the notion of information overload, appearing as one of the many forms of media in our visual environments.

Listen Carefully

Swinburne University of Technology, Faculty of Design

PRAHRAN, VICTORIA, AUSTRALIA

Class: Design Research Studio: Designer Agency
Level: Bachelor of Design Honors
Faculty: Nicki Wragg, Tony Ward, and
Keith Robertson
Duration of Project: One Semester

Listen Carefully

Students: Daniel Peterson, Samantha Austen, and Meg Phillips

PROJECT BRIEF
Students will investigate the effects of making personal (private) messages public and explore the way environmental typography can establish new channels of communication.

PROJECT GOAL
By conducting extensive research, including a literature review of cultural and media theory and a series of visual experiments focusing on the interpretation of visual/typographic messages (both private and public), students will set about collecting fragments of overheard conversations, with a view to assessing potential interpretations of these messages. Drawing into question the role of the designer in controlling the perception of messages, this project explores the notion of design as a mechanism for cultural change. It examines how the recontextualization of overheard dialogue into new forms of media alters the meaning of its message and affects those that view/interact with it.

This installation comments on existing forms of media by taking a private message and placing it in public. The stencil cutaway reveals layers of texture, color, and tone, and invites you to look closer. It reflects the density of visual communication in our urban environment and the multiplicity of meaning found beneath.

PROJECT OUTCOME
The project was achieved through a series of public installations in urban areas in Australia, based on the reinterpretation and repositioning of overheard dialogue. A continuation of the project in the form of a blog, www.listencarefully.net, invites further interpretation of the messages, allows for comment on the project, and provides an opportunity for ongoing discussion.

This installation focuses on an inherent conversation. Handcrafted and personal, this media and context creates a sense of voyeurism—that you have overheard something most private.

Adjacent to a car park and surrounded by buildings approximately six stories high, this location receives regular high-density traffic. This message is made visible to those at ground level as well as in the surrounding area, referencing road markings and challenging the audience to question the regulatory nature of our daily commute.

To confound expectation in a rapidly changing media environment, where work is painted over frequently, we opted for a return to the traditional. It's a play on preexisting visual media in a location often classified as an artist space. The message is framed, which offers alternate meanings and questions whether the message is or is not art. The positioning of this statement also calls into question the meaning of "reading," transposing it from a literary to a visual context.

The handwritten note, seemingly torn from a diary and then discarded, speaks of disposable media. The transitional nature of this media working in harmony with the nature of the message, while also drawing attention to the apparent desperation of the question, adds a degree of emotion absent from the source material.

By placing this message in a dark alleyway populated by overflowing rubbish bins, this message speaks of nothing, communicating a sense of uselessness and referencing the often vacuous nature of visual media.

Melbourne is a city of laneways and hidden locations, so directions are often a part of overheard dialogue. The recontextualization of commonly heard directions in an official media draws into question whether the message is communicating a destination or direction.

Interactive Music or Musician's Website

Temple University, Tyler School of Art

PHILADELPHIA,, PENNSYLVANIA, USA

Name of Class: Senior Interactive Design
Level: Senior
Faculty: Dermot MacCormack
Duration of Project: One Semester

PROJECT BRIEF

Create an interactive online music website that is devoted to a single musician or genre of music of your choice. The content will be decided by you, but it is recommended to keep your focus as specific as possible. This project should be an informative and educational exploration of the musician you choose, featuring links on history, tour dates, contact information, etc., as well as links to the music itself.

PROJECT GOAL

The website must integrate your initial concept(s) through the convergence of images, typography, motion, sound, and, most important, narrative. Your time during this semester will be spent between learning how to design and plan for the interactive medium and learning and expanding your knowledge of existing software; namely, Flash and After Effects. You will also place yourself in your target user's world and consider issues such as navigation, interactivity, and storytelling in a digital medium. The primary technology focus will be on advanced methods of ActionScripting, with some additional After Effects for the video component. In each case, the content can be illustrative, photographic, typographic, or QuickTime (video) and will obviously contain audio for some kind of narration. Each of your designs must be innovative and functional and at the same time allow the viewer to interact with your work. All sites must be complete.

PROJECT OUTCOME

Initially, the majority of the music websites were very playful and explorative in nature. Users were encouraged to interact and uncover the layers of content. The later projects have tended more toward describing a linear narrative, exploring a single theme. They tend to be less about interactivity and more about telling a story or delivering the lyric and music in an engaging manner.

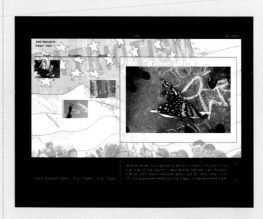

↑ **Voices of Protest**
Student: Lena Cardell

This site relates the countercultural movements from the Vietnam War era to those occurring today surrounding the war in Iraq by drawing comparisons between protest music from each decade. I selected songs that touch on three different themes: patriotism, war, and protest, and paired these themes with photography. My goal was to inform the user of the parallels between the two time periods by providing visual, textual, and aural context.

← Sun Records Legacy

Student: Al Duca

The Sun Records Legacy website offers an extensive history of the label, from its known founder, Sam Phillips, and most famous young talents, Elvis Presley and Jerry Lee Lewis, to the less famous artists and unknown facts. Its thirty-five original Sun recordings and rich, nostalgic feel reflect the grittiness of these early musical movements and encapsulate the iconic stature of the mighty record label.

↑ Alice

Student: Bomina Kim

I created an interactive CD-ROM based on an album by Tom Waits called *Alice*. The album contains the majority of songs written for the play *Alice*, based on *Alice's Adventures in Wonderland* by Lewis Carroll. I tried to capture the spirit of Waits's bizarre and dreamy lyrics and music in my illustrative work.

→ A Boy Named Sue

Student: Nick Mucilli

Hearing the tale of a "Boy Named Sue," by Johnny Cash, one can almost imagine flipping through a photo album and watching these events as they happen.

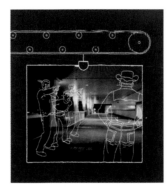

↑ Grunge Music

Student: Ronald Cala

This website acts as an introduction to the music of the early 1990s.

↑ The Man Who Couldn't Cry

Student: Scotty Reifsynder

This is a Flash animation based on the lyrics of the Johnny Cash song "The Man Who Couldn't Cry."

Beyond the Surface

Royal College of Art

LONDON, UK

Class: Passion for Print
Masters Communication Design
Level: First Year
Faculty: Richard Doust

Tutors: Richard Bonner-Morgan, Russell
Warren-Fisher, and Jeff Willis
Duration of Project: Six Weeks

PROJECT BRIEF

Through investigative research and a growing
knowledge of the possibilities of printing, you
must visually discuss your interpretation of the
meaning "beyond the surface." There will be an
ongoing need to consider how the production
processes influence your ideas en route to the
final printed work.

PROJECT GOAL

Marry the potential of print with an idea, so that
the two become equal partners, while broadening
your knowledge of the printing processes.

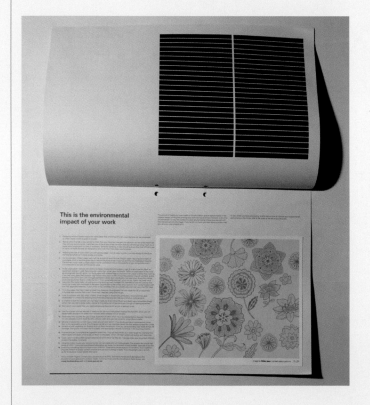

**← Lithography
Questionnaire**

Student: Lottie Crumbleholme

I always want my work to be
informative and thought provoking and to have some sort
of positive impact. I hope this
piece will teach designers
more about the print process
and make them think about
the decisions they make and
the responsibilities they have
as a designer.

↑ Carbon Fingerprint

Student: Kristina Hofmann

Environmental issues such as global warming are much talked about, but it's often difficult to take these problems seriously as the consequences are not immediately visible. Flying is an important factor in making the world a smaller place and opening our eyes to other cultures. Yet we need to be aware of the negative impact that this mode of transport has on the environment. Every time we board a plane, we significantly contribute to the greenhouse gases in our atmosphere. Air travel increasingly contributes to global warming—in more ways than one. According to the IPCC, the warming effect of aircraft emissions is about ten times that of carbon dioxide alone due to other gasses produced by planes. The fold-out poster tries to put aviation pollution in context by referencing it to other human activities. The amount of black ink covering the paper is relative to the suggested yearly allowance of carbon dioxide per person.

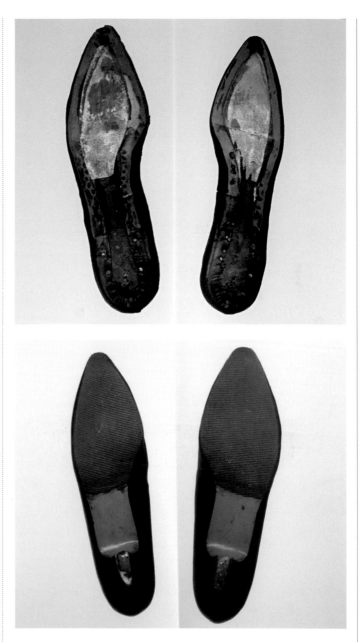

↑ Documentation of Jane

Student: Alistair Webb

The things that we interact with every day become part of a process of documentation through deterioration. This deterioration tells a story of relationships: between an object's own layers and materials and the materials, conditions, and surroundings that it finds itself interacting with and becoming a part of.

↑ The Wrong Metre

Student: Christiaan Drost

The word *metre* is from the Greek metron and its first recorded usage in English dates to 1797. The metre is a French invention and is based on one hundred thousandth of the circumference of the planet. In June 1792, the French government launched an expedition to determine the distance along the Paris meridian that ran from Dunkirk to Barcelona, so as to extrapolate to the rest of the globe. Two scientists, Jean-Baptiste-Joseph Delambre and Pierre-Francois-André Méchain were assigned to this task. Méchain measured the southern part of the meridian, and Delambre, the northern part. It took them seven years to complete this mission.

Not long before the two scientists had to present their results, Méchain came to the conclusion that he had made a mistake in his calculations. Due to this discrepancy, the metre, which was established in Paris in 1798, was short by 0.2 millimetres. Every redefinition of it has been designed to preserve the original wrong value. The discovery of this error has been quite fundamental to me; it has huge consequences for the journeys I make. I decided to show the discrepancy visually by walking along a trail the same way the scientists did more than two hundred years ago. Every kilometer is represented in two photographs printed on top of each other, one for the wrong and one for the right kilometre.

The difference in the last photograph, taken at a distance of ten kilometres (6 miles) from the start of the trail is as much as two metres (6.5 feet). The photographs are slowly revealing new landscapes that are a result of this error.

↑ The Wolf and the Seven Little Kids

Student: Elizabeth Manus

Folk stories like "The Wolf and the Seven Little Kids," collected by the Brothers Grimm, are firmly rooted in European culture. They have sprung from the collective subconscious. They are meant for people of all ages and origins. Very often, folk tales are stories of death and survival. With the help of this folk tale, I am trying to show what is actually going on in the minds of people under the smooth surface of small talk, how fundamental questions can be raised, and problems of our present time may be solved.

I started out by telling or reading the story to people and then gave them a leaflet asking them to connect their present lives to the folk tale. The story seemed to strike a chord with the reader/listener. Almost all thirty of the leaflets were returned. I selected the responses that matched key passages of the folk story and showed how individual thoughts, wishes, fears, and dreams had taken shape. This is why I left the handwritten responses and illustrations as they were. I put them on tracing paper, which let the text of the tale shine through from beneath a fleeting surface.

← Nimrod Silk 130 gsm

Student: Povilas Utovka

Revealing unknown stories about paper and destroying what I call the manifestation of discovered knowledge, I have left the surface of the paper virtually untouched.

← Television Screens

Student: Sebastian White

The project started by recording an observation. It was in the act of looking that I had found something accidentally. By using a digital camera to record a blank television monitor, one can capture something unseen by the naked eye; which is the hidden mechanics of the television screen.

The frame rate of the digital camera is much faster compared to that of the blank television monitor, and as a result, one can record the scanning beam of electrons across the screen in a pattern of horizontal lines. By varying the distance between camera and television monitor unexpected patterns and colors emerge. These patterns, caused by the varying frame rates, are known as moirés, where a ripple effect appears. The moiré pattern is usually an undesirable effect in filming as well as in printing. But for this project the moiré was welcomed.

↑ **The Eye & I**

Student: Mohammad Namazi

I decided to work with a visually impaired person, James Ridson, to discover how he sees this world. I was keen to contrast the sighted imagination versus the nonsighted one, using drawing as a tool. The different ways that the physical eye sees compared to the inner eye has always intrigued me.

The whole aim was to explore the perception of a visually impaired person of his natural and man-made surroundings and the mental images he forms of the current affairs and news that he hears. I used exactly the same pencil and paper as James did. Neither of us used any model or picture for our drawings. In my drawings, I attempted to focus more on the inner spirit of the subjects rather than the outward look or physical shape—to use the inner eye rather than the outer physical eye. I believe that this is important to get a better correlation.

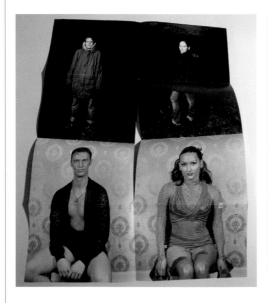

← **Alter Ego**

Student: Verena Hanschke

Additional Credit: Collaboration with Floriana Gavriel, University of the Arts, Bremen, Germany

An alter ego "the other I" is a second self, a second person within a person. German dancers Anna Walz und Domenik Herrmann reveal their alter egos: Domenik works as an insurance salesman two or three days a week, and Anna teaches dance. Before a tournament, for which they practice four to five hours a day throughout the year, they change their outward appearance dramatically. The photographs represent the deep, intense transformation of this couple.

↑ Skinned

Student: Rasha Kahil

Additional credit: Collaboration with Floriana Gavriel, University of the Arts, Bremen, Germany

What is my color? My surface consists of various colors, textures, and tones. Using a sample of each as a color in its own right, I have painted my face by numbers. I am the sum of my parts.

Pattern Magazine

University of New South Wales, College of Fine Arts

SYDNEY, NEW SOUTH WALES, AUSTRALIA

Class: Advance Typography and
Publication Design
Level: Third Year
Faculty: Ian McArthur
Duration of Project: Seven Weeks

PROJECT BRIEF

Publications are increasingly published for online access and distribution. Usually, a publication relies on writers, editors, designers, image editors, project managers/expediters, prepress checkers, advertising sales people, and a publisher. This project requires you to work as a design studio for the development of a downloadable online publication. Each of you will undertake a role within a team to develop, design, and publish an online publication. Discussion about individual design strengths and interests will assist each of you in nominating roles and developing a set of tasks you regard as appropriate for each role. The objective is to get the publication ready for online distribution in seven weeks. The focus of the publication content is up to the group to decide.

PROJECT GOAL

A downloadable screen-based publication that demonstrates appropriate typographic conventions for delivery and consumption on screen; includes promotional information and advertising in a logical sequence; and uses original photographs, montages, and illustrations The publication will conform to a set format, established by the whole group, and should be able to be output for print and screen.

PROJECT OUTCOME

Pattern Magazine can be downloaded at: http://www.staff.cofa.unsw.edu.au/~ianmcarthur/pattern_magazine/index.html

↑ *Pattern Magazine* **cover**
Student: Jenny Kong

The group selected this cover design from a range of submissions on the basis that it was appropriate but did not give a lot away in terms of referring to the visual content of the magazine.

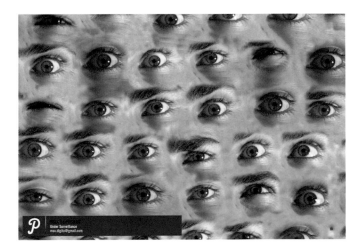

← Under Surveillance

Student: Max Lochhead

I photographed my own eye to create this slightly disturbing landscapelike piece.

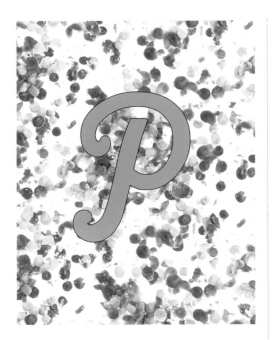

↑ Student: Anne Greader

I created this work in my bathtub by splattering brightly colored peas and corn into the water and then photographing them. It demonstrates how pattern is found in the most unexpected places, even our food. In this design, the *P* for *Pattern Magazine* can also stand for peas, hence, its green coloring.

↑ Ink

Student: Evan Papageorgiou

I developed a keen sense to graphic design as it might relate to human perception and mental health issues. This exploration of Rorschach ink blots in the context of the project looks like an early basis for his more recent work.

← Back Cover

Student: David Ing

When viewed as an Adobe PDF, the image builds itself across the screen in an apparently logical sequence of steps, reiterating the structure of the pattern.

↑ Untitled

Student: Tim Madden

Following the lead of an earlier exercise in this elective where students were asked to photograph type in the urban environment, I have applied the same idea to the project and arrived at this interpretation of the theme.

↑ Untitled

Student: David Ing

My work is often characterized by an iterative methodology. In this case, I experimented with the capabilities of Illustrator in developing seemingly random, but actually well-considered, pattern-generating approaches.

↑ Polymorphism

Student: Chao Jung Lai

I constructed this image from a hand-generated typeface featuring nine variants of each character. When assembled in various combinations, the wavelike effect seen here is created.

↑ Untitled

Student: John Holloway

I was responsible for the cod
ing behind the *Pattern Magazine* website.

lething regarded as a normative example; "the convention of not nami
isitors". 4. Something intended as a guide for making something else; "
sents problems for students of musical form"; "a visual pattern must ir
tation; "the American constitution has provided a pattern for many re;
tion of radiation from an antenna as a function of angle. 8. He path th
und O'Hare are very crowded"; "they stayed in the pattern until the fog
pattern like the ones we studied before." Pattern:1. a. A model or origin:
n, or model to be followed 1   pattern. See Synon
nisley pattern. See Syn   al or accident
n. A composite of n   ...res characteristic c   dual or a gr
..a. The configur: .unshots upon a target that   s an indic
trapnel, bomb   ots, or shot fr   otgun. 7. E   laterial t
flight pattern.   itball A pass p   r. pat-terned,   ing, pat
· previous one   sur the patt   er military can   r her fa
Pattern: noun   orth   ation or duplic   sau ide
utline of a thing,   gura   ure, form, shape   face/de
notive. See: part/whule. System   angement and   : methoc
iorder. Verb: To take as a mod: ie conform to   copy, err
follow the example of. See sar   ent/compa: ite by comb
ittern n Definition: arrangem: onyms: disord
e meanings of Pattern, see P: he pattern is a fo
inerate things or parts of a :   .pecially if tie things that are creat
ngs are said to exhibit the   . Pattern matching is the act of che
s is called pattern recognit   question of how different patterns e
· are also related to repe   pes or objects, sometimes referred t
ctly observ   ough   ses. Some patterns are named. Simpl
ular tiling ·   ie r   d balanced binary branching. The simpl
ined witho   / example, in aviation, a "hoiding pattern'
ding. Patterr   more complex when templates are usec
rb phrase) patterr, but some knowledge of the English language is rec
ogy, ethology, and Computer Science. In addition to static patterns, :
(snit)mønster, (stǿbe)model, mønster, forløb. v. tr. - tage til forbill:
efferbeeld, model waarmee gietvorm wordt gemaakt, lets n.a.v. patroo
node, modèle, patron, style, échantillon, (Ling) modèle, (Tech) modèle
ge, Schnittmuster, Strickanleitung. v. · mit Muster versehen, (nach)gest
- padrão (m), modelo (m), repetição (f) v. · padronizar, estampar, r
экрайка. Español (Spanish) n. · diseño, dibujo, motivo, estampado,
lar a imitación de, imitar, seguir el ejemplo. v. intr. · seguir el ejemp

Untitled by Rena Phuah
Obsessive repetition of floral, merging into the figures/faces as an abstract
pattern of sexuality and feminity

↑ Untitled

Student: Greta Stevens

I have a deep interest in language, so I created a pattern
from descriptions and interpretations of the term pattern
gleaned from dictionaries and
the thesaurus.

↑ Untitled

Student: Rena Phuah

"Untitled" explores notions
of femininity and sexuality
through a floral motif—like
much of my work.

Color y Carnaval

University of Bogotá Jorge Tadeo Lozano

BOGOTÁ D.C., COLOMBIA

41

Class: Basic Design
Level: First year
Faculty: Diego Giovanni Bermúdez Aguirre
Duration of Project: Six Weeks

PROJECT BRIEF

This project is based on an analytical reading of the Carnival of the city of Barranquilla (a Cultural Patrimony of Humanity, according to UNESCO) from the point of view of its overall design and its fundamental components. Each student analyzes the text for its form, color, texture, movement, and structure, relating to design as a fundamental element of the Colombian popular culture.

PROJECT GOAL

Develop color, form, structure, and space by studying the figures, masks, and dances of the Carnival of Barranquilla.

PROJECT OUTCOME

The exercise resulted in the design of a series of posters that picked up the essential elements of each aspect examined and that, moreover, were within the framework set out by the International Congress of Graphic Design, established in Merida, Venezuela, in November 2004.

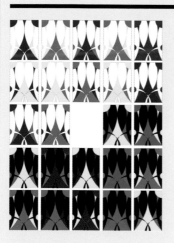

↑ **El Rey Momo**
Student: Alejandro Guerrero

The structure demonstrates the results of the analysis of the carnival text. It is the fundamental element from which comes the diverse possibilities, in terms of form and color, for the poster of King Momo.

↑ **El Congo Grande**
Student: Luisa Luna

This poster objectively expresses by means of dynamic forms and primary colors (present in the Colombian flag) the magnificence and authenticity of the Great Congo—one of the most important dances of the carnival.

↑ **El Torito**

Student: Alex Rodriguez

The Torito represents the tradition and strength of the carnival, shown in the bull-faced mask and the handling of the colors of the national flag.

↑ **La Marimonda**

Student: Laura Nieto

The Marimonda is known for gratitude and overflowing joy, elements that are expressed with complementary and warm colors.

↑ **El Monocuco**

Student: Diana Mosquera

The carnival is an example of joy and diversion through movement and spontaneity, which the poster reveals in its warm trowel of color and defined curvilinear forms.

↑ **La Negrita Puloy**

Student: Estefania Mayolo

The essential elements of the figure of the Negrita Puloy are manifested in curved forms juxtaposed with luminous colors.

↑ **El Descabezado**

Student: Carlos Mendoza

The headless Descabezado (left-without-a-leader) represents the violence lived in Colombia for decades. Asymmetry, resistance, and sharpness serve to represent this carnival personage.

The Transparent Cover

Autonomous Metropolitan University, Azcapotzako Campus

MEXICO CITY, MEXICO

42

Class: Design of Messages III
Level: Second Year
Faculty: Felix Beltran
Duration of Project: One Month

PROJECT BRIEF
Redesign the cover of the popular book *El Llano en llamas* (*The Burning Plain*) by Juan Rulfo, one of the most internationally renowned of Mexican writers. It is a book of short stories that deals with conditions of rural life at the time of the Mexican Revolution, highlighting social contrasts, the struggle for land, religion, and politics. The students have to read the book thoroughly and make assessments of the covers of previous editions. The cover trim is 4.5 × 6.5 inches (11.5 × 16.5 cm) and the printing is four color. The method for carrying out the project comprises three stages: defining the need for the design, determining the design direction, then creating the book cover.

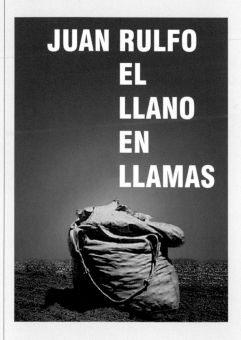

↑ Student: Carlos Rivera

↑ Student: Dulce Hernandez

The image of a half-full sack in which the harvest is deposited is evidence of the insufficiency of the production of an arid land. The glare is associated to a certain extent with a blaze and the text has a suitable contrast for readability.

This flame is awesome and devastating, and the text is placed in the space allowed by the photo. I have not reduced the size of the typography of the author's name because I consider it to be as important as the book's title.

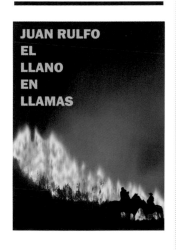

↑ Student: Christian Alvarez

I wanted to reflect the metaphor of the principal story and accentuate a dramatic scene. The heavy letters are compatible with the rest of the scene.

↑ Student: Luis Baltazar

I opted for an enflamed scene of rural workers to describe a situation that continues to exist in Mexico.

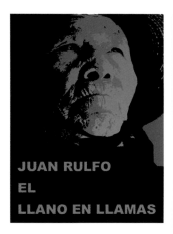

↑ Student: Liliana Linares

I decided to use a photograph of a peasant for my work, since I consider them to be the main subject of these stories. The reddish tones evoke the fire of the Mexican Revolution.

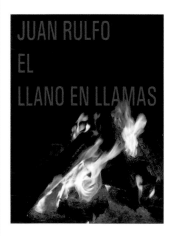

↑ Student. Elizabeth Mandujano

I decided to make the blaze more evident than that of other proposals. The peasants appearing in one corner are defenseless before the immense flames.

↑ Student: Miryam Cervantes

I tried to make the background black to accentuate the dramatic quality of the flames. The typography is condensed; I now believe it could have been a little bolder.

↑ Student: Gabriela Maciel

I wanted to reflect the conditions of the countryside described in the stories using a photograph of the peasants emerging from the blaze.

↑ Student: Jose Lopez

↑ Student: Gilda Garcia

↑ Student: Hugo Alvarez

I consider the three main defining elements of this work to be the countryside, the peasant, and the blaze. For this reason, I decided to work these three elements into a collage by which I was able to transmit the full concept of the book.

I have tried to make the flame gloomy so that it will be more consistent with the conditions in which the peasants live. The author's name is at the top to make it easy to read and the book's title is below to relate it more to that blaze growing out the arid land.

For me, more than reflecting a sudden blaze, it was important for the scene to be a metaphor for the arid, even terrible, conditions of the Mexican countryside. The typography had to stand out to help the public read it among competition from other books.

← Student: Janet Jaramillo

I tried to evoke a blaze through warm colors, because according to the assessments by the class, it was one of the most important elements for reflecting the book's contents. I did not use a photograph because I think it would be too strong. I consider the typography to be integrated with the background, but it allows suitable contrast for reading.

Reading the Urban Landscape ——————————

University of Hawai'i at Manoa, Graphic Design Program

HONOLULU, HAWAI'I, USA

PROJECT BRIEF

Senior students are assigned sites to research in the Honolulu area. These sites encompass a range of areas, including Chinatown, Manoa (a residential district), and Mapunapuna (an industrial park). Students are asked to research their sites and any typography that they find there. They then design two books (11 × 16 inches [30 × 40.5 cm]; twelve pages each—including cover) that consider the site as both a "place" and a "space" (as defined by the French literary theorist Michel de Certeau in the quotes below). The books need to work in tandem, and students are responsible for the actual content of the text as well as any images. After the books are designed, the students work together to design an exhibitionary map of the combined sites in a small student gallery. Students are asked to explore the notion of the map in its widest possible terms (conceptually and physically) as well as the unique qualities of exhibition and display. Readings on the nature of display and mapping are assigned and discussed to help students imagine possibilities. Students are responsible for the development, design, and production of the books as well as the concept, design, and implementation of the gallery installation.

"A place (*lieu*) is the order (of whatever kind) in accord with which elements are distributed in relationships of coexistence. It thus excludes the possibility of two things being in the same location (place). The law of the 'proper' rules in the place: the elements taken into consideration are beside one another, each situated in its own 'proper' and distinct location, a location it defines. A place is thus an instantaneous configuration of positions. It implies an indication of stability."   —Michel de Certeau

"A space exists when one takes into consideration vectors of direction, velocities, and time variables.

Class: Typography III
Level: Fourth Year
Faculty: Anne Bush
Duration of Project: Sixteen weeks

Thus space is composed of intersections of mobile elements. It is in a sense actuated by the ensemble of movements deployed within it. Space occurs as the effect produced by the operations that orient it, situate it, temporalize it, and make it function in a polyvalent unity of conflictual programs or contractual proximities. On this view, in the relation to place, space is like the word when it is spoken, that is, when it is caught in the ambiguity of an actualization, transformed into a term dependent upon many different conventions, situated as the act of a present (or of a time), and modified by the transformations caused by successive contexts. In contradistinction to the place, it has thus none of the univocity or stability of a 'proper.'"—Michel de Certeau

PROJECT GOAL

The goal of this project is multifaceted. Students learn to document, analyze, and interpret typography in the landscape, particularly as such typography signifies the unique identity of an urban site. They then explore the book as a typographic "site" in its own right, and in its relationship with the actual site. Extending the notion of site to a gallery space, students imagine an exhibition space as its own landscape—one that maps the relationships between all urban sites assigned in the projects and incorporates all the books. Students learn to see the urban environment and its texts as a dynamic dialogue—one that integrates public and private messages and readings.

43

← Student: Jonathan Chinen

I was assigned Liliha, an older neighborhood next to downtown Honolulu. Walking through Liliha, one sees new shops, old shops, closed shops, and condemned shops wedged within an already congested residential neighborhood. I defined Liliha as the site of a stalemate—a place defined by a "draw" between the skeletal remnants of businesses and homes with the potential for further development of the area. Spatially, people who live and work in the area respond to the site by "withdrawing"—by actively pulling back, imposing barriers and typographic signs that prohibit further encroachment. The site itself was an area outside of my own comfort zone. Visiting the site at various times of the day and night offered a valuable perspective into an area I would not have explored otherwise.

IWILEI

Student: Alban Cooper

The area in Honolulu known as Iwilei was originally an industrial shipping port but now houses, among other big-box retail stores, the largest-grossing Costco in the world. As a space of assembly, Costco allows shoppers to individually choose what they take away from the site and, in so doing, creates a kind of personal language. Through this project I realized how important it is to research and gain a sense of perspective before beginning the design.

Students: Entire Class

↑ Student: Kelli Ann Harada

These two books interpret Kaimuki as a "bypassed" neighborhood of Honolulu. As a place that has been passed by outsiders, the first book (green) examines the function of passageways and streets and how they encourage speedy travel around or through a neighborhood. The second book (blue) reinterprets the word *bypass* to be a community's passive decision to ignore modern urban development.

→ Student: Sumet Viwatmanitsakul

Downtown Honolulu houses many financial and government offices. The government seeks political power while businesses seek economic power. As a result, downtown is both a site of contention (place) and a site of promotion (space). The struggle exists between government and business (contention), but is actualized through promotion (signs and advertising in the area). I have learned that the public environment (place) is relative to how individual people use these sites (space). The two inevitably affect each other. I also learned it is essential for typography to reflect the concepts being expressed.

entrance.

A place (lieu) is the [blah blah blah blah blah blah], in accord with which elements are distributed in relationships of coexistence. It thus excludes [blah blah blah] two things being in the same location (place). The law of [blah blah blah] place: the elements taken into consideration are beside one another, each situated in its own 'proper' and distinct location, a location it defines. A place is thus [blah blah blah] configuration of positions. [blah blah blah] indication of stability.

-Michel de Certeau

Thoroughfare

→ Student: Anna Fujishige

Kapahulu is an area located between crowded Waikiki and Hawaii's main highway: H1. I have interpreted this area as a thoroughfare (place)—a way to move between the highway and Waikiki. The book was designed to make the reader move quickly through its pages. Kapahulu, however, is also a site of preservation (space) because the local residents work hard to resist the development of the area as a tourist destination. The second book was designed so that the reader would be forced to return to previous pages—to preserve what they have read. From this project I have learned that every typographical element and its particular size, layout, or spacing is always deliberate. These small elements always work together to create and enhance meaning.

Place: Kapahulu

Comic Sequence

University of Technology, Sydney

SYDNEY, NEW SOUTH WALES, AUSTRALIA

Class: Sequence and Narrative
Level: Second Year
Faculty: Sally McLaughlin and Ian Gwilt
Duration of Project: Four Weeks

PROJECT BRIEF

This four-week undergraduate project is designed to introduce second-year bachelor of design students to visual narrative. Students are asked to develop a six-frame comic sequence in response to one of the following themes: The Look, The Catch, The Scream, The Sigh, The Fall, or The End. The terms "frame" and "comic" are open to interpretation. The students are encouraged to pay attention to the narrative potential of everyday objects and events. They are also encouraged to explore the possibilities opened up by the fact that they are "showing" rather than "telling" a story. The studio work is supported by a series of four lectures. The first explores approaches to the construction of narratives, focusing on the possibilities that emerge from details of everyday life. The second explores a range of comics and graphic novel forms. The third draws on visual rhetoric as a framework for developing narrative. The final lecture considers visual hierarchy in the context of comics and graphic novels. The project is a precursor to an exploration of time-based media. In subsequent projects, students are asked to develop their narrative into a proposal for a short screen work. The proposal is realized as a storyboard and animatic.

PROJECT GOAL

The comic sequence provides us with an effective transition between our first-year print-based projects and second-year projects, many of which are screen based. Maintaining a focus on the development of a concise narrative supports the students in moving away from familiar narrative genres, toward the construction of narratives that arise from their own observations and experiences.

PROJECT OUTCOME

Comics are proving to be an interesting site for the investigation of ethical issues associated with the construction of narrative. The temptation, for a number of students, is to lean toward extreme resolutions of their sequences, resolutions that are often responded to positively by their peers. User testing is incorporated into each of the narrative projects, with a view to eliciting perspectives that extend beyond those anticipated by the students.

↑ **The Catch**

Student: Jessica Tainsh

An imaginative use of layout to convey a simple moment-to-moment narrative. At a boisterous tea party, the speaker thumps the table and a pie goes flying. The beneficiary is the baby seated at the other end.

↑ The End

Student: Michael Quill

I am trying to say no to that last glass of wine.

↑ The Scream

Student: Andrew Smith

The ubiquitous iPod. Conducive to meditation?

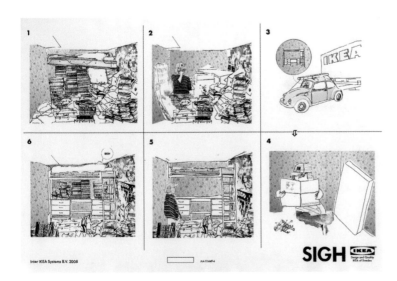

← Sigh

Student: Kinal Ladha

The frustration of assembling flat-pack furniture is suitably realized through a comic format inspired by IKEA assembly instructions.

↑ The Look

Student: Elizaveta Pogossov

A hall of mirrors sequence elicited strong responses in user testing. The sequence served as a catalyst for more general conversations about body image.

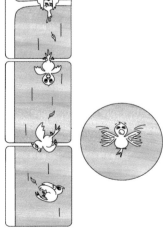

↑ The Fall

Student: Erika Forrest

A simple narrative about a baby bird leaving the nest. The challenge in the subsequent screen-based project will be to identify analogous situations that will allow the metaphorical possibilities of the sequence to emerge.

↑ The Fall

Student: Georgia Hill

An unlucky penny is the driver for this cyclical narrative.

← The Look

Student: Chris Cooper

A narrative built around the self-delusion of a would-be comic book hero, Malvolio. The sequence is realized through a series of collages. This choice of medium has created some difficulties in resolving the overall composition of the sequence and the image—text hierarchy at this stage, but the narrative structure and media exploration is effective.

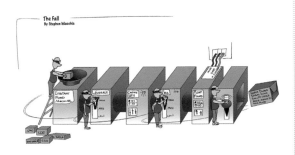

↑ The Fall

Student: Stephen Macchia

The six stages of this narrative result in a complex package of financial instruments.

↑ The Fall

Student: Carina Lee

A reflection on the persistence of the Australian drought.

Senior Degree Project in Graphic Design

The University of the Arts

PHILADELPHIA, PENNSYLVANIA, USA

45

Class: Design Studio
Level: Senior
Faculty: Ann de Forest, Kevin Finn, Nancy Mayer, Chris Myers, and Rosae Reeder
Duration of Project: One Semester

PROJECT BRIEF

This project offers you a forum to showcase writing skills, conceptual thinking, visual invention, digital and physical craftsmanship, sensitivity to audience and human factors, as well as the ability to acquire new expertise, collaborate with experts, develop self-criticism, accept diverse critique, and scale your time and resources within the scope of a complex project. Select a subject that matters to you. Frame this subject as a thesis and construct a narrative through editing exiting texts or writing an original text. This is the armature for your project. Consider issues of audience nuance that are triggered by your thesis and subject matter. Investigate and select a format and media that best expresses/explains your subject. Develop conceptual and visual strategies to support your thesis through an open, experimental process. Be responsive to audience issues. Build the narrative arc with a thoughtful, inventive, and attentive production of the artifact. The project concludes with individual, formal presentations of your project to a jury of designers and non-designers. After all of your hard work, now your job is to listen carefully.

PROJECT GOAL

The goal of this project is to fuse the multiple talents of the student in a sustained endeavor to inventively explain an issue, a subject, a text, or an idea. An understanding of narrative and storytelling structures provides the conceptual foundation for success. The initial discovery process, married to the process of making a design artifact, reveals original ways of knowing particular to each young designer. These are their new life skills.

PROJECT OUTCOME

The degree projects culminate in presentations to an invited jury of ten to twelve designers and nondesigners. These jurors determine who will be recognized for exemplary performance. Because of the comprehensive nature of the projects, they are often cited as evidence of crucial benchmarks being met by employers and graduate admission committees: among them, technical skills, inventiveness, sustained commitment, original research, writing skills, hand skills, and time management.

→ *We Are You*
Student: Johnathan Pish

This is an edited compendium of entries from military blogs written by serving soldiers and their spouses to illuminate the life of the common soldiers and their family beyond the political frame. It highlights the little things that happen during the soldiers' daily routines.

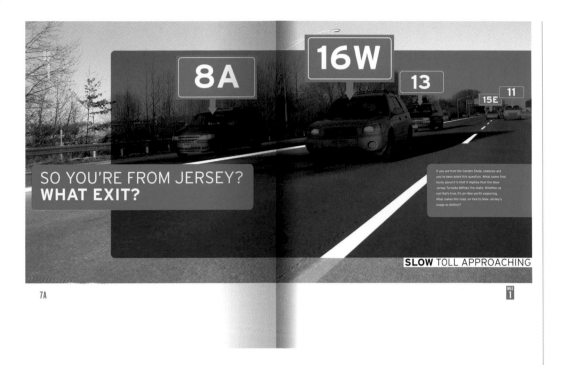

SO YOU'RE FROM JERSEY?
WHAT EXIT?

If you are from the Garden State, chances are you've been asked this question. What some find funny about it is that it implies that the New Jersey Turnpike defines the state. Whether or not that's true, it's an idea worth exploring. What makes this road, so tied to New Jersey's image so distinct?

SLOW TOLL APPROACHING

7A

MILE
1

↑ *7A*

Student: Ryan Thacker

The book is set up as a road trip, combining a running historical account of the New Jersey Turnpike with "rest stops" for various personal anecdotes and relevant asides. It is told through archival imagery, original photography, and photo illustration. Growing up in New Jersey, you essentially have two main route choices to any desirable destination, depending on what part of the state you live in: the Garden State Parkway, which runs from the southern reaches of Cape May County up the eastern part of the state to points north; or the New Jersey Turnpike, which connects the Delaware Memorial Bridge to New York City and serves as Interstate 95 through New Jersey. This means that many travelers passing through the state can do so without ever having to set eyes on scenery that does not lie within their line of sight in a speeding vehicle. This leaves out-of-staters with the notion that the New Jersey Turnpike or the Garden State Parkway *is* New Jersey, and gives rise to the "So you're from Jersey? What exit?" jokes that Garbage State residents can't escape.

This book is about standing up for something that is part of your life, for better or worse, the way you would stand up for your little brother when someone puts him down, even if you just released him from a headlock. It's about turning that joke into a point of pride, and answering proudly (in my case): *7A*.

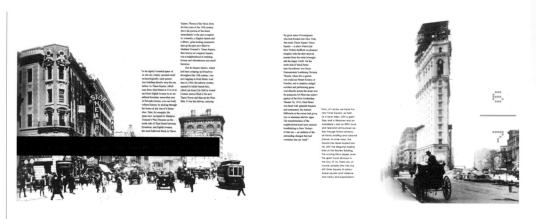

↑ *Times Square: A Conversation about Progress, Loss, Nostalgia, and Urban Vitality*

Student: Kathryn Mangano

In the past twenty years, Times Square has undergone dramatic urban remodeling, which was largely fueled by corporate investment. As public spaces are steadily shrinking, I found myself questioning if a cleaner Times Square was actually a better Times Square. I was not the only person questioning the effects of the "Disney-fication" of Times Square. As I began my research, I realized that this debate would never be properly represented by a single voice, so I assembled the book's text by weaving together five op-ed articles from outspoken and iconic New York writers. Each voice is set in its own typeface. A flexible grid was developed to allow the voices to change in volume and urgency depending on the page. Times Square's over-the-top visuals became the main inspiration for the book's design. Page numbers jump across the spreads and break all rules by changing in scale, placement, and color. Sweeping photographic imagery imparts the dizzy frenzy felt when standing at the epicenter of Times Square. Contemporary images were created by layering the photographs that I shot. The historical images were manipulated to evoke tangible environments. The book's pacing was designed to lead readers swiftly though the square's history before confronting them with today's commercial embodiment. The conversation eventually ends in a calm ambivalence. As the voices and graphics soften to trail off, the reader is left with only the promise of Times Square's transient nature.

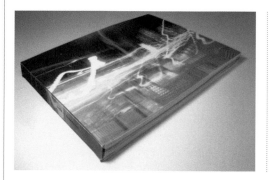

← *Life in Overdrive*

Student: Billy Mitchell

This is an edited essay and autobiographic testimony of a sufferer of ADHD and an accompanying disorder in which the patient cannot distinguish foreground and background noise. The narrative expresses hope for a cure against the odds of a daunting future.

← Soldier for a Day

Student: Nick Keppol

This collision of texts includes excerpts from Stephen Crane's *Red Badge of Courage* and an autobiographical essay. In the essay, I recount my first paintball experience and the autonomic fears that parallel Crane's protagonist, even though paintball is simulated warfare.

↑ Too Sense: The Manifesto of a Cheapskate

Student: Sean Nitchmann

I'm cheap. I'm so cheap, I'm free. That's the message of this book (and its unofficial secondary subtitle): *Liberty through Thrift*. Charged with creating an independent capstone project for my graphic design degree, I couldn't think of a more valuable use of text and image than to turn the prevailing myopic view of frugality on its head; to convey (with limited means, of course) an audaciously inspiring narrative, not disconnected at all, but cohesive, radical, and fun.

Modular Type

University of Ulster, School of Art and Design

BELFAST, UK

46

Class: Design for Visual Communication
Level: Various
Faculty: Liam McComish
Duration of Project: Two Weeks

PROJECT BRIEF

This project is designed to help students create work based on a systematic and modular approach. Students will gain improved control over composition and visual language through the systematic investigation of shape, pattern, scale, contrast, repetition, and alignment using a limited range of graphic shapes. Students were given five graphic primitives to work with.

The first part of the assignment requires researching design work that is relevant to the project, but not limited to graphic design. Then students generate letterforms using the shapes supplied in vector format using Adobe Illustrator.

PROJECT GOAL

Letters are a code for interpreting spoken language. We develop the ability to decipher this code as we grow up in our own culture. Individual typefaces are distinctive representations of this standard code and are designed in relation to centuries of custom and practice. If we wander too far from the conventions, then our ability to quickly decipher the visual code degrades. For this project, use the given graphic primitives to generate letterforms that investigate the link between shape, code, and legibility. You may scale, repeat, overlay, subtract, and add the shapes, but you must not otherwise make distortions that alter the essential proportions.

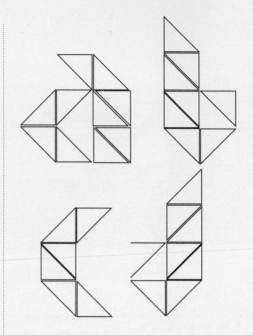

↑ Student: Peter Irvine

↑ Student: John Wynne

↓ Student: Katie Brown

↑ Student: Adam McCormick

↑ Student: Séamus Fegan

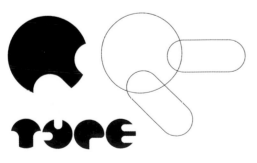

↑ Student: Ashleigh Grant

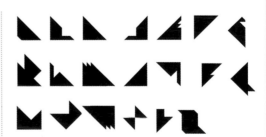

↑ Student: Ryan Stanfield

Communication Design Program

University of Washington, School of Art, Division of Design

SEATTLE, WASHINGTON, USA

Class: Communication Programs
Level: Junior
Faculty: Douglas Wadden
Duration of Project: One Quarter

PROJECT BRIEF

This course will investigate the development of a communication design program, using an international conference as an occasion to implement an array of related printed, environmental, and interactive elements that establishes the visual definition of a thematic concept as a form of graphic identity. You will base your investigations and designs on the theme of global ecologies and environmental challenges. This subject is to be researched broadly and thoroughly and should include conference presentations on climate change and global warming, energy consumption and alternate energy, species and habitat protection and management, environmental pollution and international treaties and public policy, to name just a few examples of topics that could be addressed. These, and other issues, will be presented from a national and global point of view. Your audience will be researchers and educators; representatives of nonprofit environmental institutions and foundations; international organizations; and municipal, state, and federal officials. The designs for the communication program will include: a program announcement poster; a press release and business stationery package consisting of a letterhead, business card, two envelopes, a label and folder; a nonworking prototype for a website on conference information and registration (downloadable); a prototype for site banners or a bus panel or a billboard; and a full-page black-and-white newspaper ad.

PROJECT GOAL

To investigate the development of a communication design program, using an international conference as an occasion to implement an array of related printed, environmental, and interactive elements that establishes the visual definition of a thematic concept as a form of graphic identity.

→ **Beyond the Limits: Ocean Sustainability as a Global Responsibility**
Student: Allen Lau

Beyond the Limits is a conference that focuses on the role of global thinking.

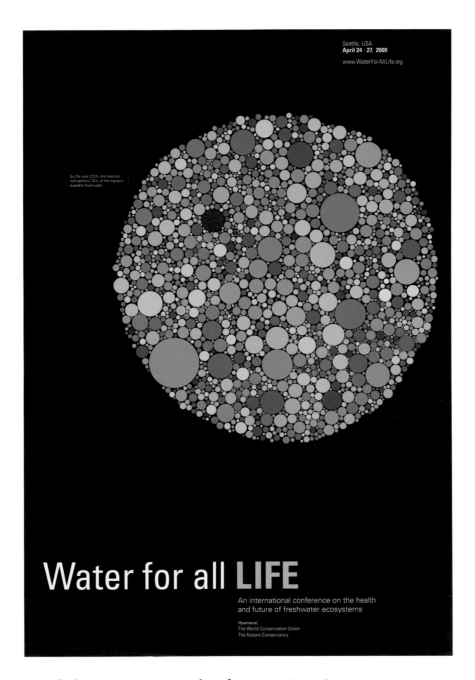

↑ Washed Away: An International Conference on Water Conservation

Student: Kayla Turner

This conference explores a hope for water conservation in domestic life. Although municipal water usage is dwarfed by agricultural and industrial usage, we must be reminded that, as individuals, we can change simple things at home to preserve our future water supply.

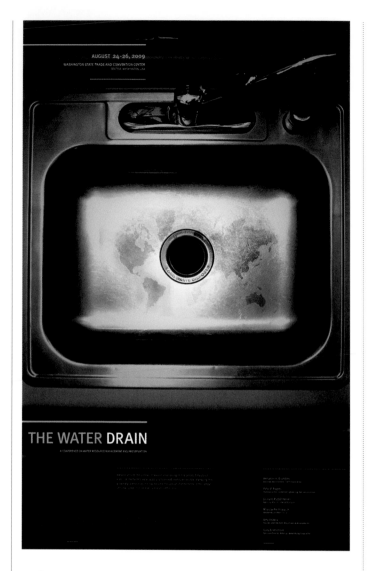

↑ The Water Drain

Student: Francis Luu

Water is vital to the survival of every human being on the planet. Less than 1 percent of the Earth's water supply is fresh and readily accessible. This brings forth the sheer importance of water management in the context of human consumption (such as nutrition, hygiene, agriculture, industrial processes, and food production). Addressing issues in regard to inefficient uses of water by humans will prove invaluable in coping with, and possibly overcoming, future catastrophes involving the scarcity of clean water, which threatens the well-being of every single person on the planet.

↑ Water for All Life

Student: Louise Foster

Humans will require 70 percent of the world's fresh water in the next twenty years, leaving only 30 percent for fresh water ecosystems. I found this statistic to be quite alarming so I decided to illustrate it in an abstract way so as not to limit the focus to one ecosystem or animal.

↑ Natural Resource Depletion

Student: Katrina Mendoza

I designed a poster, along with various applications, for a hypothetical conference about the Earth's rapidly depleting resources. I used white space to evoke a feeling of emptiness to mirror the devastation of logging and deforestation.

← Wastewater

Student: Allyson Tong

Land-based waste as a result of human activity is the largest contributor to ocean contamination. Wastewater is a conference that examines the causes of marine pollution and measures the consequences it has on ecosystems. The design of the program visually reflects the process of how oil runoff and other contaminants slowly trickle from the land and pollute the oceans.

→ Choose

Student: Mia Pizzuto

An international conference devoted to recognizing water for its original purpose, as our source of life, not death. Infectious, waterborne diseases are killing millions across the world each year. This pressing global issue must be prevented before even more innocent people become victim to this great detriment. To eliminate the risk of bacterial waterborne disease, we need to come together as a well-informed community ready to combat the problem.

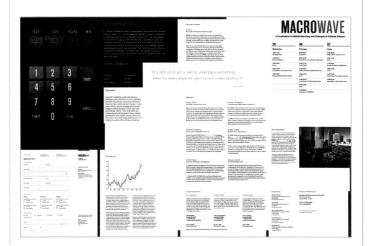

↑ Macrowave: A Conference on Global Warming

Student: Owen Irianto

I created a poster for a hypothetical conference on global warming. The functionality of the poster is based on the Swiss rationalism in which a poster should function from a distance and invite the audience to come closer, to discover what is in the details, in this case, by optical illusion. As the name of the conference suggests, Macrowave is a pun for global warming and how the greenhouse gases might affect climate changes throughout the world.

Major Design Project

University of Wollongong, Faculty of Creative Arts, School of Art and Design

WOLLONGONG, NEW SOUTH WALES, AUSTRALIA

Class: Advanced Design Project
Level: Third Year
Faculty: Grant Ellmers
Duration of Project: One Semester

PROJECT BRIEF

This subject is likely to be your final undergraduate design studio and represents the opportunity to develop a design project that encapsulates the best of your graphic design knowledge and abilities. The work should serve as a springboard for your plans after graduation. Identify your graphic design strengths and where in the industry you would like to position yourself. Allow these observations to inform the development of your design concept and the final form of your project and articulate this in a seminar presentation and written report. Support your proposal with at least three references and outline their relevance to your concept. The final project should engage with and build on the issues explored and raised in the seminar. The project should represent your design expertise and be a signature work in your design portfolio. The written report should detail your design process, references, and reflections and analysis of the final outcome.

PROJECT GOAL

The project has been developed around two components: thinking and making. Thinking occurs throughout the design process, from idea generation and formation through to completion and review. Drawing on formalized reflection, the students articulate their thinking in oral and written formats, with the aim of providing a platform that supports the transfer of knowledge to future design situations and differing contexts. Making the design process including mood boards, story-boards, design roughs, prototyping, and the final design project. Students are required to present their work to staff and peers in the following forms: an initial proposal including their design concept, research, and the intended final project form; an interim design submission that includes design roughs and concept refinement; the final design project; and a written process report. The students respond to a series of targeted questions designed to assist them stand back from the project itself and engage with the design thinking surrounding their project.

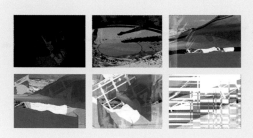

↑ No Imperfections

Student: Greg Hughes

I explore the absences of the imperfections and characteristics of analogue reproduction in a digital realm, a motion graphic work. I draw on Jacques Derrida's theory of deconstruction, specifically the terms *undecidables*, *trace*, and the *mark*. Analogue reproduction exposes these trace elements, these imperfections or characteristics within the final product, focusing on the translation or the process. This graphic approach revolves around the idea of digital reflections, the refracted leftovers from the continual analogue/digital conversions.

← Keep Your Minds Busy

Student: David Keane

Here, I look at the role of the designer as an interpreter, how a designer creates and gives meaning to words and sound. I explore this concept through the design of a poetry book with each page representing the text in an appropriate voice. I refer to the works of Guillaume Apollinaire, whose calligrammes visually evoke the text, and those of Robert Massin, who plays with the arrangement of text and image, through to designer Vince Frost and graffiti artist Banksy. My work relies on stark use of type and image, largely in black and white.

↑ Ornamental Design

Student: Dianne Cervantes

I explored the return of ornamental design as applied to wallpaper, and further investigated the repeat pattern and traditional methods of production. Issues of pattern design that I explored included the appropriation of design, the identity of the designer, and the current commercial interest in patterned wall coverings. I created a customized print for a commercial client. The design is inspired by the work of Florence Broadhurst, a noted Australian wallpaper designer and entrepreneur.

↑ Type in Motion

Student: Zoe Moxon

I created this title sequence for a fictional documentary to explore type in motion. The documentary is about Meroogal, a historical house in Nowra, Australia, that was occupied only by women from the same family from 1886 to 1985. I aimed to represent graphically the sense of history and time of the Meroogal homestead and the female occupants who lived there. The work was influenced by the title sequence work of Kyle Cooper and Animal Logic.

← **Valiant**

Student: David Wallin

This project takes a close look at the restoration and transformation of the Valiant as a means to probe issues of automotive desire. The lovingly observed visual qualities of the car are overlaid with information graphics that extend the work as a text.

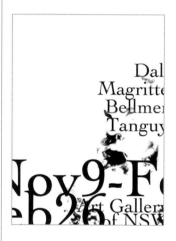

↑ **Engaging the Audience**

Student: Kate Francis

I experiment with how designers communicate with and engage an audience. I am also exploring the reader's ability to actively engage in the decoding of advertising messages, to see how little information can be provided, or pushed to the edges, before the message is unreadable. The project relies upon the reader encountering more than one of a series of images, in the city environment, in order to combine the various fragmented signifiers into a coherent whole. Visual and typographic elements give subtle clues to the reading.

↑ **Design on Film**

Student: Ben Hennessy

I explored how my own skills and sensibilities as a graphic designer could enhance the visual approach of film title sequences. The research included a survey of film titles produced by prominent graphic designers such as Saul Bass and Kyle Cooper, among others.

← Is Design Emotional?

Student: Karlee Bannon

I asked this question to investigate how a designer can establish an emotional connection with the viewer through the visual sense of typography meeting the other senses. The exploration included a series of interactive experiments and observations. One of these was to create a set of typographic prompts, which were inserted into envelopes and handed out to a group of participants. The envelope included a request for the participants to note their emotional response to the typographic prompt. From these experiments and observations, I developed a range of typographic posters that push the idea of provoking an emotional response through graphic design.

↑ Image Search

Student: Robert Dinnerville

My project sought to visualize the concepts and applications of an image search software program called Imprezzeo in a motion graphic form. The software was developed by researchers from the Universities of Wollongong and Queensland. The work serves as an eye-catching introduction for presentations to potential financial investors. My aim was to represent the key concepts behind the software in a visually engaging manner, which was achieved through the application of 2-D and 3-D modeling, motion, and sound.

→ Cultural Branding

Student: Lisa Hawkins

The 2006 Sydney New Year's event was the focal point for my exploration of cultural branding as a tool to open up interaction between participants and the event. It draws on an amusement park theme to engage audiences of all ages. The design style has adopted the already established identity of the Sydney Olympics 2000 branding and draws inspiration from Australian painters Brett Whitely and Ken Done. My design response aims to be flexible and extend into individual logos that branch off the primary logo, thus maintaining the same style in a contrasting manner. Presented here are the primary logo and secondary logo examples, applied across A2 posters and magazine advertisements.

Graphic Design with Any Media

Berlin University of the Arts/ University of Applied Arts, Institute of Design

Berlin, Germany/Vienna, Austria

Class: Graphic Design
Level: Third Semester
Faculty: Fons Hickmann
Duration of Project: Spans Several Years

PROJECT BRIEF

The projects assigned to the students explore the transgression of design limits in all respects, the critical discussion of up-to-date topics from different perspectives, the calling into question of medial and social conventions, and the development of new visual codes. The teaching concept is conceived as an ongoing enterprise, continuously spreading over several terms. Each semester, the course is entitled "Graphic Design with Any Media." It asks the students for conceptual thinking, which

is experimental and applied at the same time. (Over the course of the last years, a number of different projects have been assigned to the students.)

PROJECT GOAL

Projects that have recently been assigned to the students include: visually reacting to text-based contributions by different authors on the topic of proscriptions in the Tyrolean cultural magazine *Quart*; conceiving the graphic design concept for and realizing the production of a magazine or booklet produced as a collaborative project with students from the Berlin University of the Arts' textile and fashion design department; conceving a poster for the Berlin University of the Arts' walk-through exhibition; and designing a double-page spread for the German *Greenpeace Magazine*.

← Championship for Applied Soccer 5
Student: Astrid Seme

The graphic design class appears as initiator of the tournament and merges with the crème de la crème of international soccer.

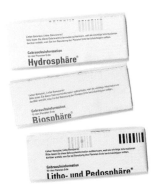

↑ Manual for Planet Earth

Student: Angelika Rattay

Four structurally and formally different directions for using planet Earth, based on texts of package inserts for medicines, deal with "adverse side effects" as well as "application" and "expiration dates." The A2 formats, conceived as newspaper supplements use illustrations and information graphics.

→ Black & White Are Infinite

Students: Karin Freinhofer, Marianne Kampel, and Mirjam Peter

"The Essence" 2006 exhibition presents a fifty-four-page brochure with selected diploma works from recent years. The profile includes eleven works and shows a wide spectrum of content, media, and methods. The take-away booklet is presented as a composition element in a gridlike wall with slits. Through moving, taking away, or adding the black and white versions of the publication, new pictures can always be generated. A built-in video provides instructions for use and invites visitors to be creative themselves.

↑ Trust Yourself

Student: Clara Bahlsen

This poster was created for the German Student Union's poster contest "Fit durchs Studium" ("Fit through studying").

Die neue Klasse Grafik. Prof. Fons Hickmann. Rundgang 20 – 22 Juli 2007
Universität der Künste Berlin

↑ **The New Class for Graphic Design**

Student: Jan Wirth

Poster for the Berlin University of the Arts' walk-through exhibition, Summer 2007. When it comes to group dynamics, networking and interaction among different actors play a specific role as part of relationships. The interdependencies, interactions, and reactions of the new class for graphic design are being typographically visualized.

↑ **A Fistful of Lead**

Student: Miriam Waszelewski

Reacting to "Sounding Lead," a contribution by Austrian psychoanalyst Elisabeth Schlebrugge on the work of artist and fellow countrywoman Eva Schlegel in the Tyrolean cultural magazine *Quart*, I take up the heaviness of the material on the pages facing the text by replacing graveness with a lighter passion for quotation.

← **Beyond Graphic Design**

Student: Christof Nardin

Beyond Graphic Design is everything but a collection of dinky little examples we're all tired of. Fons Hickmann reveals his concept of teaching and puts it up for discussion, gives impulses that provoke thoughts or even stir. He carries on asking where others would be content. The projects are not only presented, but also illustrated in the context of their intellectual background.

↑ Possibilities of Istanbul

Student: Nina Reisinger

A composition made up of contemporary Turkish poetry and visually opulent photo-collages forms a book that provides lively access to the contemporary cultural activity of Istanbul. The pictorial level opens a complex field of associations and is brought into relationship with the poems translated into English via a kind of graphic guidance system. The visual interpretation of urban space becomes like a backdrop, whereby the relationship between text and image pulsates in equilibrium on all levels of the two-hundred-page diploma work.

→ The Absolute Truth

Student: Helga Aichmaier

In the media age, the defining power of images is undisputed. But what about their authenticity, readability, and power of expression? "The Absolute Truth" illuminates the various ways in which image manipulation functions. Authentic as well as freely designed, consistently surprising contributions combined with reflective texts invite viewers to sharpen their eye for their daily consumption of pictures and develop corresponding sensitivity for the responsible handling of media.

→ Fashion Fanzine

Students: Johannes Buttner, Sabine Schwarz, Julian von Klier, Matthias Friederich, and Miriam Waszelewski

Graphic design concept for and realization of a magazine/booklet entitled *fashion fanzine*, produced as a collaborative project with students from the Berlin University of the Arts' Textile and Fashion Design Department. The publication also includes a photographic series by Johannes Buttner called "If the Kids Are United."

→ Out of the Depth of Space

Student: Sabine Schwarz

This is a visual response to articles in the Tyrolean cultural magazine *Quart* by different authors on the topic of proscriptions (or restrictions). The photographic pages facing the texts show courts, pitches, and fields, with respective regulation markings, on which a number of different games are played.

The One

Hongik University, Department of Visual Communication Design

SEOUL, KOREA

50

Class: Design Management
Level: Senior
Faculty: Don Ryun Chang
Duration of Project: One Semester

PROJECT BRIEF

The design management class at Hongik University is composed of sixty senior students who were asked to form ten teams of six members and create separate design business models based on emerging business, lifestyles, and cultural trends within the local society. The students were asked to take on individual task descriptions that vary from design, business, and management roles, with one person elected as group leader. During the course of the semester, critical paths such as scheduling, competitive analysis, product road map, design brainstorming, and media implementation plans were developed for the final outcome.

PROJECT GOAL

The primary objective is to instill the key principles of design management to senior-year design students ready to enter the profession. This project will enable them to better understand the dynamics of multilevel research, planning, team collaboration, multidisciplinary design, effective communication, and client presentation. In addition, the students are encouraged to integrate the various multidisciplinary design skill sets they have gathered during their undergraduate studies (such as illustration, photography, film, animation) and produce a holistic media presentation at the end of the semester.

PROJECT OUTCOME

The fifteen-week course is conducted with close supervision by the course professor and the final session is attended by three invited creative directors from ad agencies and design firms, who help evaluate the collective business feasibility of the ten design projects. Each year, the team with the best score is given the designation of Hongik Design Management Grand Prix. Over the years, many students who have attended this course have started their own design firms, with a more collective perspective on design management.

The project featured here was the recipient of the Grand Prix in 2004, and the team chose as their theme the increasing single household population in Korea. The group created a new lifestyle brand called "The One," which included a range of online and offline products, as well as community membership and corporate alliances with other existing companies to cater to this growing population.

CREDITS:

Team leader: Sang Min Song
Motion graphic and film: Sae Youn Koh
Product: Jung Hyun Lee
Graphic design: Hyun Kyung Yoo
Illustration: Jung Hwa Song
Film and editing: Jin Yung Park

↑ Logo

Illustration: Jung Hyun Lee

This logo communicates single life in a fun way, using an animated numeral.

↑ The One Network Partners Coupon

Illustration: Jung Hyun Lee

These coupons from various retail outlets offer special services catering to single people.

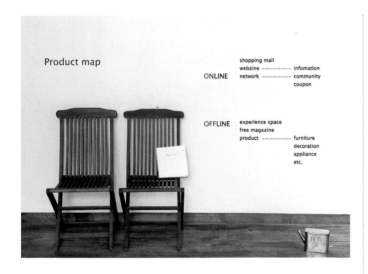

Product map

ONLINE	shopping mall webzine network	--------- Infomation --------- community coupon
OFFLINE	experience space free magazine product	--------- furniture decoration appliance etc.

↑ Product Map

Photographer: Sae Youn Koh

This page shows the product road map of the project in terms of online and offline segmentation offering contents, memberships, business alliances, and products found in experiential centers.

↑ SOS Whistle for Single Women

The whistle was designed for single women to use if they are in danger. The students produced thirty actual promotional whistles and distributed then to females in the audience during the presentation.

← Online Shop and Community Page

Photographer: Sae Youn Koh

The online shop of The One would be implemented with retail and community membership and content downloads for single members.

← Movie Trailer

We wanted to show single consumers encountering products that cater to their lifestyles and how they react to these products.

← Retail Shop

Photographer: Sae Youn Koh

Stop Global Warming

Kookmin University, College of Design

SEOUL, KOREA

PROJECT BRIEF
The idea presented to the students is to pair totally different ideas to create a poster or exhibit on how to stop global warming.

PROJECT GOAL
Create a concept using different objects and ideas and convey the concept of the urgency of global warming.

PROJECT OUTCOME
Create posters and an exhibition to travel through Korea, Japan, Thailand, and the United States.

Class: Advertising Design
Level: Third Year
Faculty: Hoseob Yoon
Duration of Project: One Semester

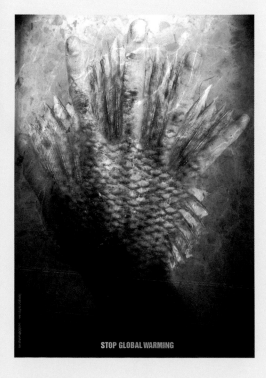

↑ **Aqua Man**
Student: Ara Yoo

↑ **No Land**
Student: Joseph Kim

↑ Save Water

Student: Bonghak Choi

↑ Steamed Earth

Student: Narae An

↑ Crucifixion

Student: Beomseok Kang

↑ Melting Lipstick

Student: Kyeonjeong Lee

↑ No Trespassing

Student: Bora Jeon

↑ Firestorm

Student: Junwoo Park

↑ Quo Vadis

Student: Mijeong Gong

↑ Under Water

Student: Suntak Kim

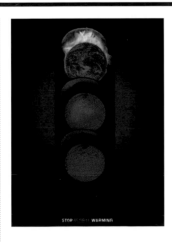

↑ Stop!

Student: Je Lee

↑ Rotten Apple

Student: Sehee Lee

Ways of Seeing (Sequential Image Making)

University of Nicosia

Nicosia, Cyprus

52

Class: Rethinking the Image
Level: Second Year
Faculty: Andreas Tomblin
Duration of Project: Four Weeks

PROJECT BRIEF

Students must choose something from the list below and produce a series of final compositions and a three-hundred-word explanation in support of the work.

1. A fly
2. A child that is lost
3. An ant
4. A cat at night
5. A spy
6. A person that has a phobia

Determine the best way to communicate through a sequence of images, which can be very simple in its concept or more complicated. For example, if the story is about love, start the brainstorming process by listing all possible love-related words—heart, chocolates, honey, sugar, sweet, bitter, jealousy, etc. This will help to establish an atmosphere and feel to the narrative. Next, develop ideas in the form of a rough-drawn storyboard. Take lots of photographs based upon the story. Consider different lighting situations and the mood they express, camera viewpoints, and so forth. (Remember, the more photographs you take, the more options you will have and the more exciting the final outcome will be.)

Students can experiment as much as they want by incorporating other objects, drawings, and writings, breaking up the images, creating photomontages, and scanning images or objects. Explore the different ways to show the following design principles within the work in order to fully communicate the ideas and observations: points of emphasis, viewpoints, ways of cropping information, scale, texture, composition, shape, color, as well as positive and negative space. Final work must be printed on good-quality paper and be presented in a folio sleeve. For the final assessment at the end of the course, all rough work must be spiral bound into one book.

GOAL OF PROJECT

The key to the problem lies in students' understanding of how different people and creatures see the world and how they can visually communicate the way in which they see. The choice of viewpoints is limitless, and there are endless opportunities to manipulate the image in relation to the way in which the subject choice sees as it relates to its surroundings and human beings. It must also be noted that students are dealing with the production of sequential, storytelling imagery, so there is a need to show this through their images. Students should think about how one image links in some way to the next one and the message they are trying to communicate.

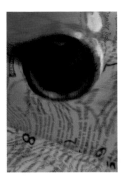   

↑ Ant Exploring a Wine Bottle

Student: Naso Kythreotou

The purpose was to explore the close-up viewpoint of an ant's perspective.

↑ Claustrophobia

Student: Panayiotis Papanicolaou

The intention was to explore the claustrophobia in a personal way.

← The Fair Ground (lost child)

Student: Stalo Panayidou

The goal was to explore personal childhood memories.

↑ Paranoia (phobia)

Student: George Klitou

The intention was to explore the phobia in an everyday setting and use the result as a basis for further research into image making.

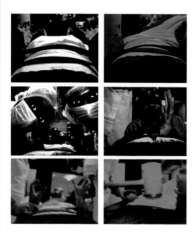

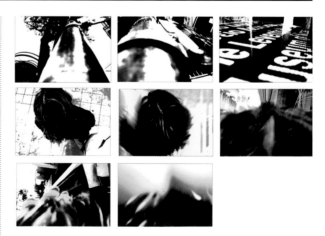

↑ Hospital Phobia

Student: Andreas Olymbios

The aim was to delve into a personal phobia.

↑ Ant Falling

Student: Andreas Neophytou

The purpose of this project was to explore the viewpoint of an ant in an urban setting.

Beatrice Warde and You

School of Visual Arts

NEW YORK, NEW YORK, USA

PROJECT BRIEF

Part 1: Read *The Crystal Goblet or Printing Should Be Invisible* by Beatrice Warde. Think about it. Formulate an opinion on the text.

Part 2: Find an additional text that responds to/reacts against/supports your beliefs in/has some relation to the *The Crystal Goblet*.

Part 3: Design a multipage document that contains both texts. Typographically show the relationship between the two texts. All text from both articles must be used, but the format (size, number of pages, etc) is up to you. You should give both texts equal conceptual weight.

PROJECT GOAL

This assignment was developed for an advanced typography class and it involved each student putting themselves in the role of editor. It also gave each of them the challenge of designing with a lot of text.

PROJECT OUTCOME

Each student took their cue from the editorial decisions they made and took the books in very different directions; the end results were quite diverse from project to project.

Class: Designing with Type
Level: Junior
Faculty: Paul Sahre
Duration of Project: Four Weeks

→ Clear Communication

Student: Sun Park

Crystal Goblet defines the role of a designer as that of enabling clear communication. But is clear communication actually possible? Does an author alone have the power to decipher the meaning of a text? Roland Barthes disputed the myth or the blind belief in the author-god by examining how readers can rewrite language/text. This double-sided fold-out poster visualizes these opposing texts on each side: On one side, *The Crystal Goblet* demonstrates that the process of book publishing (or the process of making a text sellable, from the author's initial sketch to the final format of a physical book) involves other voices such as publisher, editor, proofreader, designer, and printer. On the reverse side, I ask whether the designer, through design, doesn't also become the author of the text.

→ Beatrice Warde versus Frank Lloyd Wright
Student: Steven Attardo

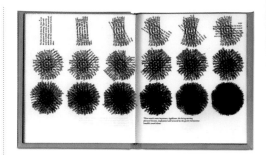

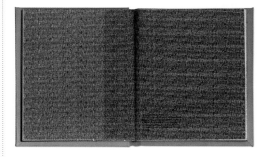

Beatrice Warde versus Frank Lloyd Wright is a book comparing two essays by two designers of a different world. Beatrice Warde said that good typography is invisible and you should not pay attention to the letters you are reading. I disagreed. I found a book of speeches by Frank Lloyd Wright that expressed his feeling that architecture should be expressive and individual. People should pay attention to the form of a building. I segmented his speech, and set it very legibly on the right-hand side of the spread. Then I set Beatrice Warde's essay to express what Frank Lloyd Wright was saying on the left. My objective was to set her essay in a way that was illegible and expressive—which is exactly what she was against.

↑ Manifesto for Growth
Student: Eric Ku

My idea for this project was to combine Beatrice Warde's essay with Bruce Mau's *An Incomplete Manifesto for Growth*. I divided Warde's text into each of Mau's forty-three manifestos, in the form of forty-three pamphlets. And although each pamphlet presents only Warde's essay, each one has its own attitude followed by the manifesto. My intent was to see the relations between those two essays.

→ High Jinks
Student: Alex Merto

The idea for this book involves rewriting and reconstructing Beatrice Warde's article in the style of e.e. cummings, and vice versa. It also includes poems that I wrote taken from Warde's essay. I liked the style of her writing, not just what she wrote about. It questions everything about written language, how it should be read and how it should be written. The result was approximately 35,000 words typeset completely on a Royal typewriter. Fitting for the styles both of Warde and e.e. cummings.

↑ House of Order

Student: Jonathan Han

Based on the crystal goblet, Beatrice Warde describes the way she sees perfect typography as clear, simple, and easy for the viewer or reader. As beautiful as what she describes typography to be, I believe that perfection, as an idea, can be reached through chaos. This allowed me the opportunity to explore typographically what it meant to refine chaos to a level of perfection.

→ *Flash*

Student: Kyi Sun

I chose to use script from the comic book *Flash Annual* for my additional text and switched the formatting of both this text and Warde's text. The resulting work was ironic because Warde wrote about how type should be neutral, but here her words are being screamed in an overtly expressive comic book format.

↓ *Two Texts*

Student: Sabine Dowek

This book compares two texts, which, in their own way, express very similar ideas. Patrick Suskind's *Perfume* is about a young man with a peculiar gift, who in his despair, travels away from Paris in search of pure air; air devoid of any human scent. On the other hand, Beatrice Warde in *The Crystal Goblet or Printing Should Be Invisible* shows her own idea of purity through typography, arguing that effective type should be transparent. When reading a book, she says, "one should never remember the typography used, but only the imagery that is a result of our imagination." Both texts search for this purity, whether in sight or scent, and they are here fused together in one book.

directory

62. Academy of Fine Arts of Bologna
Via Belle Arti 54
40100 Bologna
Italy
p: 39.051.4226411
e: info@accademiabelleartibologna.it
www.accademiabelleartibologna.it

44. Alberta College of Art and Design
1407 14th Avenue NW
Calgary, Alberta T2N 4R3
Canada
p: 403.284.7600
e: admissions@acad.ca
www.acad.ca

50. American University of Sharjah, School of Architecture and Design
PO Box 26666
Sharjah, Emirate of Sharjah 26666
United Arab Emirates
p: 971.6.515.2807
e: aberbic@aus.edu
www.aus.edu

56. Art Center College of Design
1700 Lida Street
Pasadena, CA 91103
USA
p: 626.396.2200
e: nik.hafermaas@artcenter.edu
www.artcenter.edu/gpk

74. Arts Academy of Split, Department of Visual Communications
Glagoljaska bb
21000 Split
Croatia
p: 385.21.348.622
e: design@umas.hr
www.umas.hr/dvk10

40. The Arts Institute at Bournemouth
Wallisdown
Poole, Dorset BH12 5HH
UK
p: 44.1202.363.305
e: khardie@aib.ac.uk
www.aib.ac.uk

180. Autonomous Metropolitan University, Azcapotzako Campus
Avenida San Pablo 180
Mexico, D.F. 02200
Mexico
p: 52.55.53189175
e: jdepin@correo.azc.uam.mx
www.azc.uam.mx

60, 206. Berlin University of the Arts
PO Box 120544
10595 Berlin
Germany
p: 49.30.2450
e: presse@udk-berlin.de
www.udk-berlin.de

65. Boston University, School of Visual Arts
855 Commonwealth Avenue
Boston, MA 02215
USA
p: 617.353.3371
e: visuarts@bu.edu
www.bu.edu/cfa/visual-arts

68. Brigham Young University
Provo, UT 84602
USA
p: 801.422.4266
www.visualarts.byu.edu

82. Fabrica, the Benetton Group Communications Research Center
Villa Pastega, Via Ferrarezza
Catena di Villorba
31020 Treviso
Italy
p: 39.422.516111
e: fabrica@fabrica.it
www.fabrica.it

130. Folkwang University Essen
Universitätsstrasse 12
45117 Essen
Germany
p: 49.201.183.3607
e: ralf@dejong-typografie.de
www.folkwang-hochschule.de

210. Hongik University, Department of Visual Communication Design
72-1 Sangsu-dong, Mapo-gu
Seoul 121-791
Korea
p: 82.2.320.1114
www.hongik.ac.kr/english_neo

88. Iceland Academy of the Arts
Skipholt 1
105 Reykjavik
Iceland
p: 354.699.0580
e: lhi@lhi.is
www.lhi.is

92. Illinois Institute of Technology, Institute of Design
350 North LaSalle Drive
Chicago, IL 60654
USA
p: 312.595.4900
e: design@id.iit.edu
www.id.iit.edu

94. Istanbul Bilgi University, Department of Visual Communication Design
Eski Silahtaraga Elektrik Santrali
Kazim Karabekir Caddesi 1, Silahtar
Mahallesi Sütlüce, Eyüp
34060 Istanbul
Turkey
p: 90.212.311.5000
e: vcd@bilgi.edu.tr
vcd.bilgi.edu.tr

122. Jan Matejko Academy of Fine Arts, Faculty of Industrial Design, Department of Visual Communication
Plac Matejki 13
31-157 Kraków
Poland
p: 48.12.299.2000
e: rektor@asp.krakow.pl
www.asp.krakow.pl

213. Kookmin University, College of Design
861-1 Jeongneung-dong Seongbuk-gu
136 702 Seoul
Korea
p: 82.2.910.4583
e: english.kookmin.ac.kr/

34. London College of Communication
Elephant and Castle
London SE1 6SB
UK
p: 44.20.7.514.6569
e: info@lcc.arts.ac.uk
www.lcc.arts.ac.uk

28. Maryland Institute College of Art
1300 Mt. Royal Avenue
Baltimore, MD 21210
USA
p: 410.225.2222
www.mica.edu

78. Maryse Eloy School of Art
Rue Bouvier 1
75011 Paris
France
p: +33 158 39 36 60
e: eme@ecole-maryse-eloy.com
www.ecole-maryse-eloy.com

106. Massachusetts College of Art and Design
621 Huntington Avenue
Boston, MA 02115
USA
p: 617.879.7000
e: admissions@massart.edu
www.massart.edu

110. Missouri State University, Department of Art and Design
901 South National Avenue
Springfield, MO 65897
USA
p: 417.836.5110
e: artanddesign@missouristate.edu
art.missouristate.edu

114. North Carolina State University, College of Design
PO Box 7701
Brooks Hall
Raleigh, North Carolina 27695
USA.
p: 919.515.8322
e: design@ncsu.edu
ncsudesign.org/content

126. Portfolio Center
125 Bennett Street
Atlanta, GA 30309
USA
p: 404.351.5055
e: hank@portfoliocenter.com
www.portfoliocenter.com

86. Red and Yellow School of Logic and Magic
40 Sir Lowry Road Central
Cape Town, Western Cape 8001
South Africa
p: 27.21.462.1946
e: hazel@redandyellow.co.za
www.redandyellow.co.za

134. Rhode Island School of Design
Two College Street
Providence, RI 02903
USA
p: 401.454.6100
e: webmaster@risd.edu
www.risdgd.com

138. RMIT University, The Works, Communication Design
GPO Box 2476V
Melbourne, Victoria 3001
Australia
p: 61.3.9925.1243
e: russell.kerr@rmit.edu.au
www.theworksdesign.com.au

168. Royal College of Art
Kensington Gore
London SW7 2EU
UK
p: 44.20.7590.4304
e: richard.doust@rca.ac.uk
www.rca.ac.uk

140. School of the Art Institute of Chicago
37 South Wabash Avenue
Chicago, IL 60603
USA.
p: 312.629.6100
p: admiss@saic.edu
www.saic.edu

152, 219. School of Visual Arts
209 East 23rd Street
New York, NY 10010
U.S.A.
p: 212.592.2600
e: mfa.design@sva.edu
www.design.sva.edu

144. Senac University Center, Santo Amaro Campus
Avenida Eng. Eusébio Stevaux 823
São Paulo 04696-000
Brazil
p: 55.11.5682.7300
e: campussantoamaro@sp.senac.br
www.sp.senac.br/cas

149. State University of New York, Purchase College, School of Art and Design
Visual Arts Building, 735 Anderson
Hill Road
Purchase, NY 10577
USA
p: 914.251.6750
www.purchase.edu

86. Stellenbosch University
Private Bag X1
Matieland, Western Cape 7602
South Africa
p: 27.21.808.9111
e: seb@sun.ac.za
www.sun.ac.za

65. Suzhou Art and Design Technology Institute
Wuzhong Building
189 Zhineng Road North
Suzhou International Park
Suzhou, Soochow
China
p: 512.6650.0118
www.sgmart.com

162, 164. Swinburne University of Technology, Faculty of Design
Building PA, 144 High Street
Prahran, Victoria 3181
Australia
p: 61.3.9214.6880
e: nwragg@swin.edu.au
www.swinburne.edu.au/design

166. Temple University, Tyler School of Art
7725 Penrose Avenue
Philadelphia, PA 19122
USA
p: 215.777.9000
e: tyler@temple.edu
www.temple.edu/tyler

78. University of Art and Design Helsinki
Hämeentie 135 C
00560 Helsinki
Finland
p: 358.9.75631
e: info@taik.fi
www.taik.fi

178. University of Bogotá Jorge Tadeo Lozano
Carrera 422-61
Bogotá D.C. 11001
Colombia
p: 571.3341777
e: diseno.grafico@utadeo.edu.co
www.utadeo.edu.co

103. University IUAV of Venice, Department of Art & Industrial Design
Ex-Convento delle Terese
Dorsoduro 2206
30123 Venice
Italy
p: 39.42.2415882
e: medicaldesign@iuav.it
www.iuav.it/medicaldesign

183. University of Hawai'i at Manoa, Graphic Design Program
2535 McCarthy Mall
Honolulu, HI 96822
USA
p: 808.956.8251
e: design@hawaii.edu
www.hawaii.edu/art

38. University of Ljubljana, Academy of Fine Arts and Design
Erjavceva 23
1000 Ljubljana, Slovenia
p: 386.1.427.21.26
e: alu-design@aluo.uni-lj.si
www.alu.uni-lj.si/

174. University of New South Wales, College of Fine Arts
Greens Road, Paddington
Sydney, New South Wales 2021
Australia
p: 61.2 .9385.0684
e: cofa@unsw.edu.au
www.cofa.unsw.edu.au

216. University of Nicosia
PO Box 24005
1700 Nicosia
Cyprus
p: 357.2.2841500
e: toblin.a.@unic.ac.cy
www.unic.ac.cy

188. University of Technology, Sydney
PO Box 123
Broadway, New South Wales 2007
p: 61.2.9514.2000
e: dab.info@uts.edu.au
www.dab.uts.edu.au

206. University of the Applied Arts, Institute of Design
Oskar Kokoschka Platz 2
1010 Vienna
Austria
p: 43.1.71133.2411
e: pr@uni-ak.ac.at
www.dleangewandte.at/design

118, 192. The University of the Arts
320 South Broad Street
Philadelphia, PA 19102
USA
p: 800.616.ARTS
e: info@uarts.edu
www.uarts.edu

196. University of Ulster, School of Art and Design
Belfast Campus, York Street
Belfast BT15 1ED
UK
p: 44.28.90267265
e: l.mccomish@ulster.ac.uk
www.ulster.ac.uk

198. University of Washington, School of Art, Division of Design
102 Stevens Way
Seattle, WA 98195
USA
p: 206.543.0970
e: uaskart@u.washington.edu
www.art.washington.edu

202. University of Wollongong. Faculty of Creative Arts, School of Art & Design
Northfields Avenue
Wollongong, New South Wales 2522
Australia
p: 61.2.4221.5853
e: tanyab@uow.edu.au
www.uow.edu.au/crearts/sad/

30. Virginia Commonwealth University, School of the Arts in Qatar
PO Box 8095
Doha, Qatar
p: 974.551.9747
e: pphatanateacha@qatar.vcu.edu
www.qatar.vcu.edu

100. Yildiz Technical University, Department of Communication Design
Besiktas Central Campus, Barbaros Bulvari
34349 Istanbul
Turkey
p: 90.212.383.2731
e: oozcan@yildiz.edu.tr
www.ilet.yildiz.edu.tr